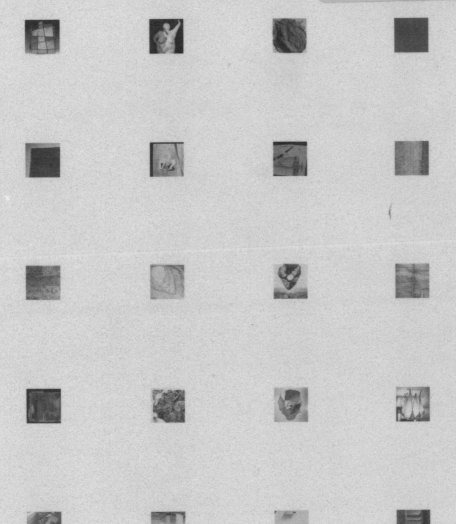

ARTISANS

PAPER

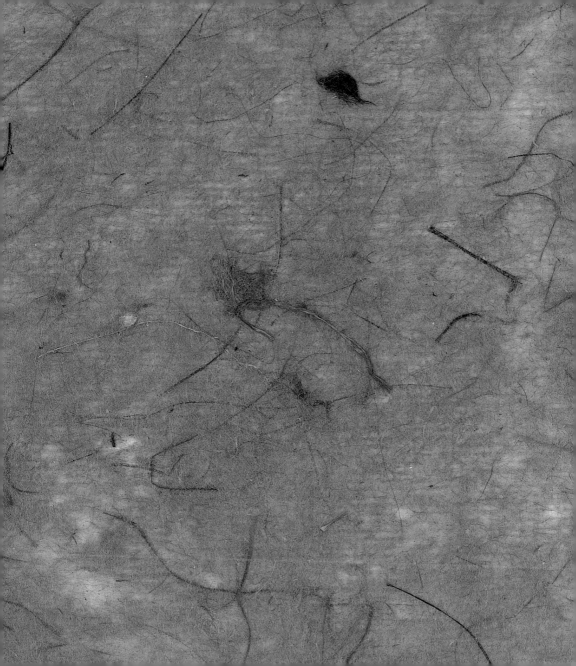

ARTISANS

PAPER

AN INSPIRATIONAL PORTFOLIO

GABRIELLE FALKINER

Watson-Guptill Publications
New York

Copyright © 1999 The Ivy Press

First published in the United States in 1999
by Watson-Guptill Publications,
a division of BPI Communications, Inc.,
1515 Broadway, New York, NY 10036

Editorial Director: Sophie Collins
Managing Editor: Anne Townley
Project Editor: Sorrel Everton
Editor: Lindsay McTeague
Art Director: Peter Bridgewater
Designer: Alan Osbahr
Photographer: Richard Waite
Picture Researcher: Liz Eddison

Library of Congress Catalog Card Number:
99-60389

ISBN: 0-8230-0304-3

This book was conceived, designed,
produced, and first published
in the United Kingdom in 1999
by THE IVY PRESS LIMITED
2/3 St. Andrews Place
Lewes, East Sussex BN7 1UP

Reproduction and Printing in Hong Kong by
Hong Kong Graphic and Printing Ltd.

Above: Spiral by Inger-Johanne Brautaset, 1998
p.144: Exhibition by Kyoko Ibe, 1997/98
Cover: Money 1997 by Therese Weber, 1997

CONTENTS

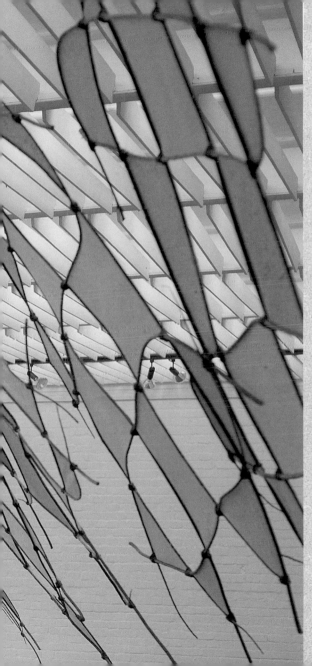

Lightbeam

6½ft x 6½ft x variable
length (2m x 2m x
variable length)

Jane Balsgaard
1989

INTRODUCTION

The art of making paper was

discovered over two thousand years

ago in the Far East and, with the

growth in written communication that

it heralded, it helped shape the

world as we now know it. This

section follows the history of one

of the most influential "chance"

inventions, from its beginnings to its

current importance worldwide.

PAPER

Paper was first invented in China, supposedly by accident, when rotting rags in a pool of water were stirred up and trampled on by passing feet and finally left drying out in a hot, dry summer to produce a strange, stiff piece of material on which marks could be made with a chalky stone or charcoal. The idea was developed a step further with ropes and fishing nets being beaten to a pulp with water. The pulp was then drained, pressed into sheets, and allowed to dry in the sun. Papermaking as a process was formally introduced at the Chinese court in CE 105 by the court eunuch Ts'ai Lun, although there is archaeological evidence that paper was probably made almost 200 years earlier than this.

When the Chinese first realized what a useful material they had discovered they closely guarded the secrets of how to make it, and appear to have succeeded until the seventh century, when the craft was being practiced in Korea and Japan. The first evidence of paper being mass produced was in 770 in Japan, when the Empress Shotoku ordered the printing of a million *dharani*, or prayers. Each paper prayer was encased in a carved wooden pagoda, and the pagodas were lodged in temples throughout the country. The material used to make the paper for this ambitious project was hemp, which makes a strong and lasting sheet—some of the prayers still exist today.

The Chinese Empire spread across Asia and included the city of Samarkand. In 751 the city—along with its papermakers—was captured from the Chinese by the proselytizing soldiers of Islam. Thus the knowledge of papermaking finally escaped from the Chinese and moved westward, some 650 years after the process of papermaking had first been formalized. The Arabs were in no doubt about the benefits of this new material and made use of it to help spread the word of Muhammad. The expansion of Islam over the next 300 years took the knowledge of papermaking through the Middle East and into Europe.

The earliest records of papermaking in Europe are in Spain, in the twelfth century, in the region around Valencia and Toledo, which at that time was under Islamic rule. Gradually, papermaking skills spread

Paper can be described simply as a thin layer of intertwined fibers caught in a sievelike screen. Here the papermaker continues the process by turning the fresh sheet of paper out of the mold in preparation for pressing and drying.

north through Spain and into the rest of Europe. One of the earliest
known documents, currently in the Bibliothèque Nationale in Paris, is
a Visigothic manuscript of the twelfth century from Silos near Burgos in
northern Spain. The earliest royal document written on paper is a deed
of King Roger of Sicily in southern Italy written in the year 1102.
Interestingly, there are no records of early manuscripts on paper from
Greece, probably because at that time the country was still part of
the Byzantine Empire and—without the influence of Islam—was not
yet using paper.

The first mill

As papermaking skills moved north through Italy, the first paper mill for
which records exist was founded at Fabriano in 1276—and it still exists
today. The mill is now the largest of the many papermakers in Italy,
producing all kinds of paper from a small but excellent range of
handmade sheets, for artists and fine letterpress printing, to various
grades for commercial use, including the paper for the Italian currency.

    With many mills established in the northern part of Italy, the
supply of paper over the Alps into northern Europe was assured. One
of the earliest examples of paper in official use in England is a register
of the hustings court at Lyme Regis, on the coast of Dorset, which has its
first entry dated 1309. This paper is similar to the paper that came from
Spain at the same time. The earliest examples of blotting paper, first
mentioned in 1476, have been found as fragments between the leaves
of fifteenth-century account books. Before this, sand—an abundant and
free commodity—was sprinkled over ink to help it dry.

    Papermaking on a serious commercial scale was not established
in England until the end of the fifteenth century, when John Tate set up a
mill in Hertfordshire. The mill supplied paper to the printer Wynkyn de
Worde, who had taken over the workshop of Caxton and later moved
the business near to St. Paul's Cathedral, London. John Tate's business,
however, did not survive, perhaps falling victim to competition from the

Continent. In Europe, the middle of the fifteenth century saw the first printing with movable type, by Johann Gutenberg in Germany, which was to lead to a great expansion of literacy and, therefore, a demand for paper. This demand was further fueled the following century during the Reformation of the western Christian Church, when numerous copies of the Bible were printed in the vernacular. It was not long before there was a shortage of paper.

Since paper was made from hemp, cotton, and linen rags, people were encouraged to save all available scraps of these materials. Eventually, in 1666, a law was passed in England forbidding the burial of any corpse in a shroud made of these fabrics—only wool could be used. As a result, more than 220,000lb (100,000kg) of cotton, linen, and hemp rag were saved each year to be used for papermaking.

Until the end of the seventeenth century all the paper used in what was to become the United States was imported from Europe, but in 1690 the first mill was built by William Rittenhouse near Germantown, Pennsylvania. This first mill was built of logs and was destroyed by floods in 1700. The new Rittenhouse Mill was built a short distance away, this time of stone; all that remains of it today is the mill house with a stone over one of the windows with the inscription CWB 1707.

A developing industry

A further mill was established by Thomas Willcox in about 1729 on the west branch of Chester Creek, also in Pennsylvania. Willcox, an immigrant from Devon in England, brought with him cuttings of ivy which he grew over the mill, so giving the mill its name—"Ivy Mills." An ivy leaf was also used as a watermark to identify where the paper came from. This mill made paper used for currency notes and was exported to South America as well as to Europe, supplying banks in Greece.

The first mill known in the New York area was established by Hendrick Onderdonk on Silver Lake, in Roslyn, Long Island. The mill prospered and Onderdonk became a leading member of the local

This plate showing the activities of a paper mill comes from Diderot's *L'Encyclopèdie*, published in France c.1760. Here, a post of newly formed sheets of paper is being pressed while another worker processes the paper pulp.

community. In 1790 he invited President George Washington to breakfast. Tradition has it that the president was taken on a tour of the mill to watch paper being made and that he tried his hand at forming a sheet—although no evidence that this really happened now exists.

By 1810 it is reckoned that there were up to 185 paper mills established, but virtually all hand papermaking had been superseded by machine by the end of the Civil War.

When papermaking first developed, the product was primarily used for the written word, but soon artists were using paper and the earliest wood engravings used as book illustrations date from the fifteenth century. As techniques improved it was possible to make special papers for specific purposes.

Today, the vast majority of high-quality papers for artists and for fine printing are made entirely or partly from cotton linters, which is the part of the cotton boll that is not suitable for spinning into thread for weaving. Papers now available include 100 percent cotton paper for commercial stationery, which is at the top end of the market, and drawing and printing papers, which have a cotton content added to the pulp.

The French artist Ingres gave his name to a particular type of drawing paper which he favored and today Ingres-type paper is made by a number of mills. The Arches Mill in France makes an excellent ingres-type paper that contains as much as 25 percent cotton. Watercolor, cartridge, cover, and copying all describe differing grades of paper for various uses—the quality determined by the pulp content.

After its virtual disappearance as a skill, the craft of hand papermaking is returning. Over the last 50 years, interest in the history of making paper by hand has quickly developed into using paper to create works of art. Today there are many commercial ventures making and selling handmade papers.

MATERIALS

Paper is made from plant fibers,

or cellulose. Any plant, if prepared

in the correct way, can be used to

make paper, and the more cellulose

the original material contains, the

better the quality of finished paper.

In this section we look at how the

basic materials are processed, in

methods unchanged for centuries,

to form a sheet of paper.

An old washing machine motor is converted to serve as a beater for preparing pulp for making paper.

PAPER

A range of raw materials that can be used in the papermaking process—old rags, cotton linters, wood—anything with a good fibrous content.

THE BASIC INGREDIENTS

The earliest papers of which we have evidence were mostly made from hemp (*Cannabis sativa*), which is once again being grown for papermaking. Hemp is a good material since it yields a high proportion of long, strong cellulose fibers. It can be used on its own or it can be combined with other materials, such as cotton (*Gossypium*), linen (*Linum usitatissimum*), or wood pulp.

Cotton, linen, and hemp were all used for papermaking before the development of wood pulp, but today cotton is found only in sheets of the highest quality paper, made specifically for artists and other craftworkers. The stems of the flax plant are used to make the linen, which is still a component of specialized papers made for work on the conservation of documents.

Most modern paper for everyday use starts life as a tree, grown in a sustainable forest. The trees are logged and transported to a paper mill, where they are turned into wood pulp. Developments in technology have made it possible to remove the lignin from the pulp, resulting in what is called wood-free, or acid-free, paper, which is durable. It is the lignin that reacts with the atmosphere, causing paper to decay over time. "Archival" paper is expected to have a life of at least 200 years.

Oriental papermaking, in countries such as Japan, China, Thailand, and other Far Eastern countries, obtains its raw materials from suitable indigenous plants. In Japan the most important plant is the paper mulberry, or *kozo* (*Broussonetia papyriferia*). *Kozo* has long fibers, producing strong sheets of paper that are particularly useful for any purpose requiring lightness with strength and possibly translucency.

Other Oriental plants include *gampi* (*Wikstroemia sikokiana*), which grows in the wild and cannot be cultivated. The resulting paper can either be exceedingly thin and transparent or thick and almost like vellum. *Mitsumata* (*Edgeworthia papyriferia*) belongs to the same family as *gampi* and produces paper that has the most beautiful sheen.

FROM PLANT TO PULP

To produce high-quality paper from basic materials, such as cotton rags, the rags must first be reduced to a pulp. The clean rags should be torn into bite-sized pieces removing any foreign matter, such as buttons. Colored rags are also removed unless a special shade of paper is required. The pieces of rag are then boiled in a lye, or solution, of caustic soda or other alkaline chemical to break down the plant material and release the cellulose fibers. Depending on the quality of the rag, boiling can take up to 24 hours. Pulp made from cotton linters (the short fibers from around the cotton seed) takes much less time to prepare.

Following the cooking, which produces a coarse pulp, the material is drained and rinsed to remove all traces of caustic soda before being treated in a Hollander beater to completely separate the fibers that form each thread from one another. The Hollander, which was invented in the late seventeenth century, consists of a large oval tub partly divided longitudinally down the middle. In one half is a cylindrical roller, which is covered in rows of sharpened metal bars. It sits above, but doesn't touch, a series of sharpened metal bedplates attached to the floor of the tub. As the roller rotates, the coarse pulp, mixed with water, is rubbed or torn against the bedplates and then circulates around the tub and back to the roller. After a thorough beating the pulp will feel slightly slimy and slippery and is ready for the next stage. The pulp, now known as "stuff," is diluted with large quantities of water and transferred to the stuff chest where it is stored, ready for use in the papermaking vat.

The purpose of beating is to ensure a fine pulp with no lumps but without beating the components so much that all the fiber length and strength of the material is lost. It is a combination of the raw materials and how they are treated at each stage in the process that gives each kind of paper its own characteristics. For example, the paper Pergamenata (Italian for parchment) is very hard and has a translucent quality that is acquired by beating the pulp much more than normal.

THE VAT AND THE MOLD AND DECKLE

The prepared pulp is transferred by pump or gravity feed from the stuff chest to the papermaking vat. Here it is mixed with fresh water prior to forming the first sheets of paper—the ratio of pulp to water governs the thickness of the sheets of paper in a given make. The vat is kept agitated so that the fibers of the papermaking material remain evenly dispersed in the water.

To form a sheet of paper, the craftworker, known as the vatman, uses a mold and deckle. The basic mold is a rectangular frame—the size of which dictates the dimensions of the piece of paper—with mesh stretched over the top to form a "cover" on which the piece of paper is made. A professional's mold is made of hardwood with brass bindings, and a mesh of fine bronze wire. The joints are formed with the greatest care and the whole is designed so that it will not warp.

The deckle is a detachable frame, about 1 in (2.5cm) high, that fits over the mold and restrains the paper pulp as each sheet is formed. The vatman holds the deckle over the mold and dips the mold into the vat, lifts it, and dexterously shakes it so that the pulp forms an even layer over the wire mesh. The mold is placed on the horn (also known as the stay), a shelf at the side of the vat to drain, and the deckle is carefully removed so that no water falls onto the newly formed sheet. Even a single spot of water will result in a blemish in the finished paper. In a process known as couching (pronounced "cooching"), the wet sheet is then transferred from the mold, rather like turning a cake out of its tin, onto a dampened felt, or piece of blanket, larger than the sheet. Meanwhile, the vatman is forming the next sheet which, in turn, is couched onto a felt laid on top of the previous wet sheet. A pile of new wet sheets interleaved with felts is called a post.

Oriental papermaking uses essentially the same technique but there are differences that reflect the materials used and the style of the finished sheet of paper. These Oriental techniques are discussed in their own section (see pages 44–51).

The vatman skillfully lifts the mold and deckle from the vat leaving an even layer of pulp on the mesh. Handmade paper does not have a distinct fiber direction because this technique creates an intermingling of fibers going every way.

PRESSES AND SIZING

Pressing is used at various stages in paper production. When making handmade paper, a post of wet sheets, interleaved with felts, is normally pressed in a hydraulically operated press (known as the squeeze) to remove excess water and facilitate binding of the fibers.

Following the initial pressing, the wet sheets are separated and divided according to the desired final finish. For a rough surface the sheets are hung in a large airy room, either on big sheets of burlap or over ropes to air dry in the draft, which is allowed into the room through its slatted sides. On average, it takes between one and seven days for the sheets to dry, depending on climatic conditions.

For a lightly textured, or cold-pressed surface, the sheets are put back in a press between felts and allowed to dry under light pressure for anything up to 12 hours. To achieve a smooth, or hot-pressed, surface the paper is pressed between hot sheets of zinc or between heated rollers. Hot pressing is, however, highly skilled. Unless the sheets are loaded very carefully, the edges are easily damaged.

Dried sheets of handmade paper, known as waterleaf, may need to be finished, or sized, with a protective coating. Without sizing, fluid ink or paint will bleed, or feather, on the paper, as the fibers absorb the liquid. Some sizes are added to the pulp during beating (known as internal sizing), while others are applied to the finished sheet (surface sizing). All commercial papers are sized internally.

Many different materials can be used for sizing, including rice starch (in Oriental papermaking), the juices of various plants, gelatine, and synthetic resins. The simplest method of sizing handmade paper is to make a size bath of gelatine and water in a large tray and dip the sheets of paper in the solution, before pressing and drying again. Gelatine sizing, which is the most traditional, gives a hard surface to the sheet which means that a very fine line that does not bleed can be made and color can be carefully controlled. For this reason it is ideally suited to watercolor papers. Other vegetable-based and pH neutral premixed sizes are now available and are widely used.

The top and bottom sheets shown are examples of laid paper. Laid lines running the length of the paper are clearly seen in the bottom sheet. On the top sheet, chain lines are visible running at right angles to the laid lines. The middle sheet is an example of a wove paper without lines.

LAID AND WOVE PAPER

Before about 1750 all European and American handmade paper—machines had not yet been invented—was made on "laid" molds, the same style of mold that today's handmade papermakers use. The mesh of the laid mold cover is made of closely spaced thin wires stretched along the length of the mold, which form fine lines, known as laid lines, in the finished sheet of paper. The thin wires are held in place with stronger wires at regular intervals of ½–1¼in (1–3cm) across the breadth of the mold. These lines, at right angles to the laid lines, are called chain lines because of their appearance. A sheet of paper with clearly defined laid and chain lines, visible when the sheet is held up to the light, is called laid paper.

In about 1750, Englishman John Baskerville, the renowned Birmingham printer, devised a way of weaving the mold cover so that no lines appeared in the sheet. This type of paper is called wove paper. Today it is mostly a matter of fashion and personal preference whether laid or wove paper is chosen for a particular printing job.

Modern machinemade paper can be made to look laid on one side. This appearance is created during manufacture by applying a top roller—the dandy roll—along the length of the paper. The roller is constructed to give the familiar laid look to a sheet, usually with the chain lines running in the direction of the grain of the paper.

Nearly all Oriental papers made by hand are laid; this is caused by the strengthening chain lines woven into the closely woven bamboo material of the *su* (mold cover).

The Fourdrinier in action
producing a continuous web of
paper without the need for any
human involvement.

MACHINEMADE AND MOLD-MADE PAPER

Until the end of the eighteenth century all paper was made by hand, but the invention of the first papermaking machine by Nicholas-Louis Robert was to have a profound effect on the industry. Robert, an inventive mechanic, was working at Essonnes in France as inspector of personnel in a paper mill owned by François Didot. At the time, the mill was experiencing labor problems and Robert and Didot realized that the development of a machine would be of tremendous benefit to the business.

The first trials were not entirely fruitful but, following more experiments, the first successful sheets of paper were formed mechanically in 1797. The machine worked by pouring a continuous stream of paper pulp onto a moving wire mesh or mold, like a conveyor belt. This vibrated, spreading the pulp and allowing the excess water to drain away before passing the wet sheet between felt rollers to partially dry it. At the end of the process the sheet was lifted from the machine and torn along a tear line made by the cutting bar, which gave a natural-looking torn edge to the sheet. The paper was then hung to dry in the normal way.

Patents were applied for, but because of arguments with his patron, Robert never benefited fully from his invention. Meanwhile Didot had contacted his brother-in-law, John Gamble, an English papermaker, who discussed the project with the London stationers Henry and Sealy Fourdrinier. The brothers built a larger machine along the lines of Robert's invention and to this day the machine is known as a Fourdrinier.

Jets evenly distribute a fine spray
of pulp onto the cylinder from
where it is transferred to a
rotating loop of felt.

However, although they patented the machine, the Fourdriniers did not receive any royalties because of a flaw in the patent.

Mold-made paper, contrary to what its name suggests, is not made in a traditional mold but on a rotating cylinder with a wire mesh on the outer surface. In early cylinder machines, the partially submerged cylinder revolved in a vat of pulp and the water was sucked away from the inside of the cylinder, leaving a mat of fibers on the outer cloth. As this came to the top of the vat, it was transferred to a continuous moving felt, from where it passed over and under rollers which squeezed out excess water until a completed sheet of paper could be lifted off at the dry end of the machine. All mold-made paper has two deckle edges, formed where the pulp is restrained at the edge of the wire mesh, and—to the untrained eye—appears to be handmade.

In the modern process, pulp is sprayed onto the cylinder, rather than being picked up from a vat. Present-day machines make paper as wide as 5ft (1.5m), and the sheets can also be produced in a continuous web. Alternatively, the papermaking machine can be set to separate the sheets of paper at a given length. If imperial size watercolor paper is being made, the machine will be set for the tear line to appear every 30in (76cm).

Both mold-made and machinemade papers—unlike handmade paper—have a distinct grain direction. The faster the papermaking machine runs, the more fibers are pulled into the path of the rollers, which means that sheets taken from the machine will fold more easily in the direction in which they have been made than across it.

TECHNIQUES

It was not until the middle of the

twentieth century that artists began

to see paper as an inspirational

material in its own right. Even a

flat piece of paper can vary in

color, pattern, and texture. But

paper is also infinitely versatile—it

falls, folds, and rustles, it leads the

artist in how it should be formed,

and it can be pulped and remade

into new and exciting shapes.

Colored pulp is
scattered to create
a vibrant image.

PAPER

COLOR IN PAPER

The earliest papers were probably all white or—more likely—off-white, but color has been added to paper for centuries. There is now an enormous range of different colored and patterned papers available, ranging from single-hued handmade sheets and those with multicolored speckles to the almost infinite selection of commercially produced patterned wrapping papers.

The first coloring agents were natural dyes obtained from natural objects, such as berries, bark, peat, red chalk, turmeric, and verdigris. Because they were generally not colorfast, the dyes were often fixed with a solvent such as salt, vinegar, or even urine, added to the pulp along with the dye. These natural colors are still favored for particular uses such as in paper used for conservation, or in other instances where a natural, traditional look is required. Instead of using dyes directly, handmade papers of cotton rag can be tinted by using colored cotton to make the pulp. Old denim, for example, makes a strong paper in a lovely shade of pale blue.

Today, however, most machinemade colored papers are achieved with commercial chemical dyes. For the most part these colorings are not lightfast and, in some cases, the color may eventually fade entirely, which means that it is advisable to keep all artwork made of paper or on paper away from direct sunlight. If a single color is required, this is added to the pulp in the beater, while for a multicolored pattern the design is printed onto the paper.

With their uneven structure, rough deckled edge, and variation of tone, colored papers currently imported from Nepal afford endless opportunities to the paper artist. Handmade colored paper from Japan has been available for many years and is a favorite with printmakers, picture framers, and paper artists. Since it is fairly soft, it has a pleasant way of falling into elegant folds when suspended and the texture in the paper comes into play, affecting its apparent color.

All these pieces are examples of colored and patterned European papers. From left to right: brown tissue paper with woodgrain printed pattern; printed pattern paper from paper publisher Judd Street Gallery; gold-coated paper; another printed pattern paper from Judd Street Gallery; Marlmarque—an American text paper; Dutch printed pattern paper; and finally, two examples of Parchmarque text paper.

This particular piece of marbled paper is a popular design known as Peacock, or Bouquet. It is very popular among Italian makers of marbled paper.

MARBLING

The earliest known examples of marbling on paper are from Japan, and date from the early twelfth century. The Japanese technique continues to be practiced today and is known as *suminagashi*, or the art of floating color. Spots of water-based inks are sprinkled onto a bath or basin containing water mixed with a size of gum tragacanth, which supports the colors. Then the spots of color are carefully drawn out using a fine wooden pin or spatula to form an irregular pattern of spiraling lines somewhat like the map contours of a mountainous area. A sheet of paper is placed on the surface of the water and then carefully lifted off to reveal an abstract design covering the entire sheet.

The Persians marbled the boards of some of their manuscripts using random stone patterns, achieved by leaving the spots of color untouched, or with swirling patterns made by combing the colors into curls and waves. This pale, gentle style is still practiced in India, where much hand-marbled paper is produced today.

West European travelers to Turkey in the sixteenth century discovered the skill of marbling and took it home with them. The first marbled papers used in England were imported from Holland—the earliest known example is on a binding dated 1655. To avoid paying tax on the imported material, it was used as wrapping paper for toys, for example, then smoothed out, ironed, and used by bookbinders. Almost invariably the pattern was the same, a combed wave—now known as nonpareil—which was further teased into curls and known since its origin as Old Dutch. By 1670 the papers were in regular use.

Various marbled patterns continued to be popular throughout the nineteenth century, with bookbinders traditionally making their own marbled papers. During the first half of the twentieth century, however, marbling went out of fashion and it was almost impossible to obtain marbled papers. The skill was largely kept alive in Hertfordshire, England, in the workshop of Douglas Cockerell and his son and successor Sydney, who died in 1987. Gradually interest and demand returned, the old recipes were rediscovered, and marbling enjoyed its renaissance.

Today there are several workshops making hand-marbled papers for a wide variety of applications, although by far the most common use to which they are put is as the covers and endpapers of books.

Marbling techniques

There are two basic methods for marbling paper. The first, which tends to create a soft outline between the colors and a gentle effect no matter how deep the tones, involves using oil-based colors. They are combed into a pattern on the surface of a bath of water and transferred to a sheet of paper by lowering it onto the pattern. The paper is lifted and set aside to dry while the color is cleared from the bath by skimming it off the surface. The pattern is then recreated and the process repeated. It is not possible to make more than one sheet from each application of color, because as soon as the sheet is lowered and then removed from the surface, the colors are displaced. This means that no two pieces of hand-marbled paper are completely identical—each one is a monoprint—which is why marblers charge a copyright fee for the reproduction of one of their creations.

The second, and perhaps more popular, method is to use a size, or water-resistant material, on which to marble. A gelatinous size of carrageen moss is used to support water-based colors. The paper to be marbled is dampened in a size of alum so that the colors will take and the wet sheet is carefully lowered onto the marbled carrageen size. Once the pattern has transferred, the sheet is rinsed with clean water to remove excess color before being hung to dry. The variety of patterns that can be obtained by this method is immense. The marbler will usually mix four colors in one design to balance the variation between light and dark and give pleasing tonal gradations.

A technique known as *ebru*, or floating clouds, developed in Turkey between the twelfth and thirteenth centuries, is again being widely studied and practiced. Using a size of gum tragacanth and pale colors, marblers can create figurative patterns, such as flowers and clouds, and form them into pictures, which can be framed with abstract marbling.

The paper rests briefly on the surface of the water, just long enough for the colors to be transferred, and is then carefully lifted off, rinsed, and left to dry.

ADDITIONAL MATERIALS

With the increased interest in all craft processes, many papermakers are now experimenting with fibers other than the more traditional cotton, linen, hemp, and wood pulp, with interesting results.

One of the first exponents of this approach was John Mason, who taught papermaking as part of the printmaking course at Leicester Polytechnic, England, in the 1950s. He took groups of students to forage for papermaking plants, such as nettles and bracken. At his studio at the Ten by Eight Press he proved that paper could be made from almost any plant—it is just that some are more suitable than others.

There are now several papermakers who make decorative sheets, which are then incorporated in other works of craftsmanship, such as book covers or even text pages and printmaking sheets. These papermakers use both recycled materials, such as paper, cotton rag, and old wool socks, and plants found growing locally. Modern hand papermaking in India has produced a wide range of papers utilizing material other than tailor's waste. Recycled burlap bags, for example, usually made from jute, produce a beautiful, naturally toned paper.

For both texture and color, raw plant fibers can be added to the basic materials at various stages in the process. The Gmund Mill in Bavaria uses recycled cotton and straw to produce a range of papers that look almost handmade, with tiny bits of bark and straw showing. The name of the range, "The Naturals," reflects the look of the sheets of paper, yet they are entirely suited to modern printing methods.

Small flowers, petals, strands of grass, and fronds of fern are all used to create "Inclusions Florales," a handmade paper by Richard de Bas of Ambert in France. The wildflower mixture is gathered fresh each morning during the summer months and strewn over the newly formed sheets of handmade paper before they are couched. The papermaker gives an extra shake to the mold just to allow a tiny bit of pulp to trap the plant fragments, which are then pressed firmly onto the sheet as it is dried. Indian papermakers produce similar sheets—in two weights—which have a slightly more primitive appeal.

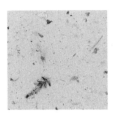

Almost anything can be added to paper pulp. Strips of thick paper will add tone and texture to the sheet shown in preparation on the facing page, while the sheet above, contains fronds from a fern.

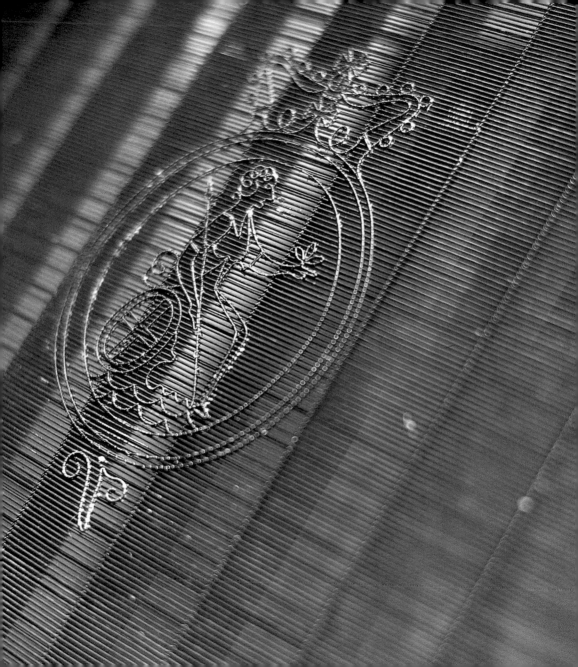

WATERMARKS

Watermarks are the patterns or devices which can be seen in a sheet of paper held up to the light, and which identify the mill or the papermaker from which the sheet originates. They are known as watermarks because they are invariably introduced while the paper is in its pulp state.

The first watermarks in European paper appeared in Spain in about 1151 and in Italy more than a hundred years later. In some cases certain marks came to denote particular sizes of paper, thus the fool's cap and bell mark gave its name—foolscap—to a sheet measuring 13in x 17in (330mm x 432mm). This size was later known as Double Cap and the fool's cap mark was replaced by the Britannia mark.

Watermarks are made by creating the required shape out of wire, then embroidering it carefully on to the wire cover of the mold. Words are embroidered directly on the mold cover. Good examples of modern watermarks—well designed and with a crisp outline—can be found in some of the papers made in the Fabriano mill in Italy and in the papers of Saunders Waterford, together with others from the St. Cuthbert's Mill in Somerset, England.

Artists normally regard a watermark in the middle of a sheet of paper as intrusive, so most modern watermarked paper has this identification on the edge. Many artists, particularly printmakers, like to have a special paper made for them, carrying their own watermark, usually a representation of their signature—Picasso, Motherwell, and Miró, for example, all had their own papers made. This can be useful in establishing the authenticity of a piece if it is known that the original edition was printed on a specially watermarked paper.

When a paper is machinemade, the watermark is added by means of a dandy roll. The roll, which has the mark embroidered on it, runs over the paper while it is formed on the felt and before it passes between the drying rolls of the machine.

The Britannia watermark (left) was used to denote foolscap paper and was used by many mills in England. The mold shown here is an old one. The watermark shown above is used to denote paper from Griffen Mill, England. The "MC" relates to the mill's proprietors; the infinity mark shows that the paper is permanent, while the "GM" identifies Griffen Mill.

From bottom to top. *Hatsukoi—*
handmade paper with fibers
and gold flecks; *Tanabata
unryu*—black with gold and
silver flecks; screen-printed
paper of black and gold
squares; *Asarakusui—*
machinemade, lacy sheet,
Matsuyuki—machinemade tissue
paper with gold and silver
flecks; *Shoin*—machinemade
paper of tiny squares;
Tanabata—pink sheet with gold
and silver flecks and fibers;
Unryu—handmade textured
paper with strands of glass fiber.

JAPANESE PAPERMAKING

Traditionally, papermaking in Japan is a winter task carried out by
farmers when they cannot get onto their land. The most important
papermaking plants come from the *kozo* family, which grow to over
6ft (1.8m) tall and are harvested in autumn. The cut stems are tied into
manageable bundles and steamed in a closed compartment over an
enormous copper to loosen the bark. The stems are then hammered and
the bark is stripped off and dried. The remaining wood is used as fuel.

To separate the layers of bark into the inner white growth and
the unwanted outer black layer, the bark is soaked in running water and
"treaded" (trampled on) until softened. A sharp knife is used to ease the
white from the black and then, with a piece in each hand, they are
pulled away from each other. The fewer black specks remaining on the
white, the better the quality of the finished paper. It is important that all
the bark in a batch should be from the same quality of growth—bark
from fast-growing young shoots is the most valuable. The cleaned white
fiber, known as bast, is dried and baled ready for sale to the
papermaker, who prepares pulp from it.

Dried bast is soaked for up to two days in pH neutral water
(water that is neither acid nor alkaline) then cooked with either caustic
soda or sodium carbonate, chemicals which have almost entirely
replaced the traditional potash made from a lye of wood ash. Cooking
separates the cellulose fiber from the lignin and other constituents of the
raw material. The amount of cooking and the proportion of chemicals to
bast are factors in determining the quality and style of the finished paper.
After cooking, the now fine strands of kozo are carefully drained and
washed, and any remaining black specks of impurity are removed.

Preparing the pulp

Beating the prepared bast to make pulp would originally have been
done by hand with a heavy mallet, and was later superseded by trip
hammers operated by people or by water power. Now the Japanese

have altered the Hollander beater by replacing the heavy roller, which in Western papermaking macerates the cotton or linen fibers, with curved blades. These are an adaptation of the traditional fighting halberd, which gives its name, *naginata*, to the device. The hooked blades gently tear the fibers apart to make a fine papermaking pulp that will not form lumps in the vat. Once the pulp is ready, it can be kept wet but must not be allowed to ferment.

To hold the long fine fibers in place in the finished sheet, *neri* is added to the pulp. *Neri*, which means sticky or viscous, is made from the root of the tororo-aoi plant (*Abelmoschus monihot medikug* or *Hibiscus manihot L.*), which is boiled to extract its sizelike quality. The cooked, softened root is hammered to a pulp and a small amount added to the papermaking vat at regular intervals. It gives the sheet added strength, as well as prevents the fibers from clumping together.

In Japan, sheets of handmade paper are often much larger than those normally made in the West, so the mold is supported by a gantry of bamboo poles, which take its weight when it is loaded. Another slight variation is that the deckle is an integral part of the mold, which is itself lined with an inner layer, the *su*. The *su* is very like the mesh cover on a Western mold, but it is formed from thin bamboo strips instead of wire and it is lifted from the mold with the newly formed sheet still on it to be transferred directly to the post without the need for interleaving felts.

The Japanese word for Western-style papermaking is *tame-zuki* —literally, "the fill-and-hold way to make paper." This neatly describes the manner in which a conventional mold and deckle are dipped into the vat then lifted and shaken to distribute the pulp evenly across the mesh of the mold. The word for the Japanese method is *nagashi-zuki*— "to flow and slosh to make paper," an equally apt description.

The big-handled mold, supported on its gantry of bamboo poles, is dipped into the vat and the pulp is made to flow forward in a wave across the *su*. Further waves are added to the sheet before it is couched onto the post of wet sheets. The completed post is pressed and the sheets are separated onto drying boards.

The mold is supported as it is dipped into the vat. The vatman subjects the pulp to a series of shakes and waves, more than one dipping and a final throwing off of any excess pulp before the *su* is transferred to the post.

NEPALESE AND INDIAN PAPERMAKING

Paper has been made in Nepal for more than 1,500 years, and it is in this region that it is still made by what was probably the first method to be developed in ancient China.

The Nepalese use an indigenous group of plants, known locally as *loktha*, for papermaking fiber. These plants grow freely under the forest canopy and are various species of daphne and edgeworthia, both from the *Thymelaeaceae* family. There was a period when deforestation for fuel caused a shortage of *loktha*, but now that the forest is being ecologically managed the *loktha* has been reestablished. It is cropped on an annual basis, much as *kozo* is in Japan.

Paper is frequently made close to the place where the raw material grows. The bast fiber is prepared by stripping the plant and cooking it, before pounding it with sledgehammers on a stone mortar. The prepared pulp is rolled into small balls, each sufficient for one sheet. A mountain stream is diverted into an improvised vat, often made from a hollowed log. To make a sheet, the papermaker—usually a woman— takes a ball of pulp and breaks it up into a container of water. This diluted pulp is then carefully poured onto a simple mold made by covering a frame with a loosely woven cloth and securing it with wooden pegs. By floating the mold on top of the water in the vat, the pulp is spread to form a sheet. The mold is then lifted from the vat, given a gentle shake to settle the fibers and placed in the sun to dry.

Drying takes about two hours, then the newly formed sheets are piled into a post, weighted down with heavy stones to press them, and, once they have finished drying, folded ready for transportation either within Nepal or off the mountains to find their way into Western stationers.

The *nagashi-zuki* Japanese method of papermaking is now also carried out in Nepal, but because it is still a somewhat primitive exercise

here and it would not be practical to carry heavy machinery into the mountains, a few minor adaptations have been made: the *su* has an underlining of silk, rather than bamboo, and the cooked bast is beaten with mallets, not in a mechanical beater.

Indian methods

Papermaking must have reached India via Nepal and Kashmir as a result of the Mongol invasion of the subcontinent during the twelfth century. There is no certain date for the introduction of the skill, but the Khagzi, the traditional papermakers of northern India, are Muslim, and there is still a tradition of Muslim papermaking at Sunganer, near Jaipur.

Paper is made on a *chapri*, a flexible screen woven from strong grass stems not unlike the fine bamboo *su* used in Japan. The *chapri* is laid onto a simple mold and the deckle is controlled by fixed front and back runners and two separate side pieces of wood held in place by the papermaker as the sheet is formed. The sheets are couched one on top of the other before being brushed onto smooth plaster walls to dry. The slightly curved chain lines on the finished paper are created when the *chapri* is lifted from its supporting frame before the sheet is couched.

The present-day papermaking skills of southern India were promoted by Gandhi and today provide a great deal of employment, as well as produce some beautiful paper. Much of the industry uses recycled cotton waste from the clothing business as its raw material. High-quality watercolor paper, together with cotton sheets to which other fibers have been added, are a staple of the trade. Asters and calendula petals and little pieces of grass embedded in the sheets are often added to make an attractive background for special uses, for example, as invitations. Banana leaf fibers make elegant brown sheets and the fibers of bagasse (sugar cane) give a yellow-tan sheet. Algae fibers from the waterways yield greenish paper.

A selection of Nepalese colored and textured papers. From left to right: Wild banana paper with strands of banana fiber visible; Nepalese fine tissue paper with *loktha* fibers; variously colored tissues, some smooth, some textured; heavy tissue with bamboo leaves caught in the surface.

Layers and blocks of colored pulp are built up on a freely draining base to create a strongly textured piece. Preparing the pulps individually gives a depth of color that cannot be achieved by simply adding dyes to the surface of the work.

TWO- AND THREE-DIMENSIONAL WORKS OF ART

All the works featured in the gallery section of this book (pp57–139) are made from or constructed from paper. The very flexibility of paper as a medium means that the distinction between art and craft can become blurred. The works featured here show that paper, when used as an artistic medium in itself, falls beyond the scope of painting and printmaking and is usually related to installation..art.

Neither origami—the highly skilled Oriental art of folding paper to form sculptural objects—nor papier-mâché have been included in the gallery section, since both are craft mediums in their own right. There are examples of sculptural works that do look like papier-mâché, but the essential difference is that while with papier-mâché a piece is built up of layers of paper pasted or glued together to make the thickness of material required, paper works rely for their strength on the size in the pulp.

The content of the paper artworks shown here depends on the imagination and emotions of the artist, who has a wide range of tools and materials to choose from in order to achieve the desired effect. The Japanese artist Kyoko Ibe (see page 90) utilizes the natural materials of her culture's papermaking tradition to create enormous works often using bamboo poles and pure dyed *kozo* pulp to form her preplanned images. She says of the nature of her work, "I do not make paper...It's like putting down a color on a bamboo canvas."

Sometimes a paper artwork is created to explain another process, such as degradation—one of Elizabeth Stuart Smith's installation pieces is a good example. It takes the form of a series of containers made from pure brown kraft paper, each of which holds other paper material. The containers were arranged decoratively in a public park, then photographed over a period of time to note their natural degeneration. Thus the interaction of the material with the environment was measured over time and the record forms a photographic journal. Other works may recycle high-quality printmaking or watercolor paper, often making use of trimmings and offcuts. These can be repulped, dyes added to give the paper integral color, and used to create an entirely

different material. This is evident in the abstract images made by the artist David Watson from rectangles of differently colored re-formed pulps (see page 53).

In order to work like this, artists have to be imaginative about the tools as well as the materials they employ, and the ability to improvise is essential. Strips of paper and water can be quickly reduced to a pulp in a domestic food processor in order to recycle paper and, for larger-scale projects, an old washing-machine motor can be used to power a homemade beater. Brian Richardson, who is married to Maureen Richardson, a paper artist who works in Herefordshire, England, has written a paper on how to adapt a sink waste disposal unit for this purpose.

In the piece shown here, David Watson recycled paper, coloring the pulp vivid green and yellow with hot-water fabric dye, which gives a very strong tone. He then tore the finished sheets into strips about 4in (10cm) wide before reshaping them to form his paper work. He used an old band-saw blade not only to add to the artistic response to the piece but also to fix and define the outline of the work in its curved shape.

The wide range of work featured in the gallery section of this book gives some indication of the many other materials that may be used in the construction of these pieces. Some are freestanding, others are supported. Because the color is often within the material, not applied separately, it can give great depth and a certain intensity to the work—an intensity that can be enhanced by the use of light. To take just a few examples, Helen Hiebert (see page 88) has used individually colored sheets to form plant-inspired sculptural lamps, while Catherine Nash from Arizona (see page 106) takes her inspiration from her oceanside upbringing in New England and her present desert environment, with work that displays the influences of both and emphasizes the similarities of two very different experiences of great space.

The ease with which paper can be combined with other materials in two- and three-dimensional works allows the artist free rein in conveying his or her inspiration.

GALLERY

A growing number of contemporary artists are turning to paper as the perfect medium for expressing and evoking an infinite range of emotions. This gallery highlights just some of the varied, exciting, and innovative work that paper artisans are creating from this natural material.

Shiuka kozo fiber papers 42½ft x 104½ft (13m x 32m), 141 Building, Sendai, Japan. Kyoko Ibe 1992

JANE BALSGAARD

Since the completion of her education at the Royal Danish Academy of Art in Copenhagen, Jane Balsgaard has exhibited her work extensively in Europe and Japan. The inspiration behind her delicate structures, such as the one shown here, came while creating prototypes for large-scale exhibition pieces of iron and sisal paper. But in the end, it was the smaller structures that obsessed her. These miniature pieces are of the lightest-weight materials—stick skeletons, partly covered with paper made of plants from Balsgaard's garden and seaweed from the coast; their delicacy enhanced by the translucency of the paper.

Construction
1¼ft x 1ft x ½ft (35cm x 30cm x 15cm)
Jane Balsgaard 1997

MY STRUCTURES ARE METAPHORS FOR SMALL CABINS, BOATS, AND PRIMITIVE CONSTRUCTIONS. BUT I AM NOT RESTRICTED IN THE WAY AN ARCHITECT IS, I AM FREE TO FOLLOW THE DIRECTIONS AND EXPRESSION IN THE WAY THE STICKS CURVE INTO EACH OTHER.

LUCIA BARATA

Lucia Barata, whose roots are in the cultures of North Africa and South America, was raised in an atmosphere sympathetic to the visual arts and music. Following training in architecture in Rio de Janeiro, Brazil, where she specialized in drawing, painting, papermaking, and art therapy, she expanded her professional skills to also encompass interior and graphic design. For 16 years she combined her professional life as an architect/designer with her activities as an artist, but finally her desire to create works of art triumphed. In 1991 she moved to Rome and developed her ideas for working in paper, exploring its strengths and weaknesses and expanded her plans for future works in this material.

Big Mama
5½ft x 3ft x 2¼ft (170cm x 90cm x 70cm)
Lucia Barata 1998

WHILE IN BRAZIL MY QUEST HAD ALWAYS BEEN FOR THE ETERNAL. MY FIRST MEMORIES ABOUT PAPER COME FROM PLAY DURING MY CHILDHOOD. AND PAPER WAS ALWAYS THERE, IN THE MUSIC BOOKS FROM WHICH I STUDIED PIANO, IN THE BOOKS I READ TO MY POORLY SIGHTED GRANDMA.

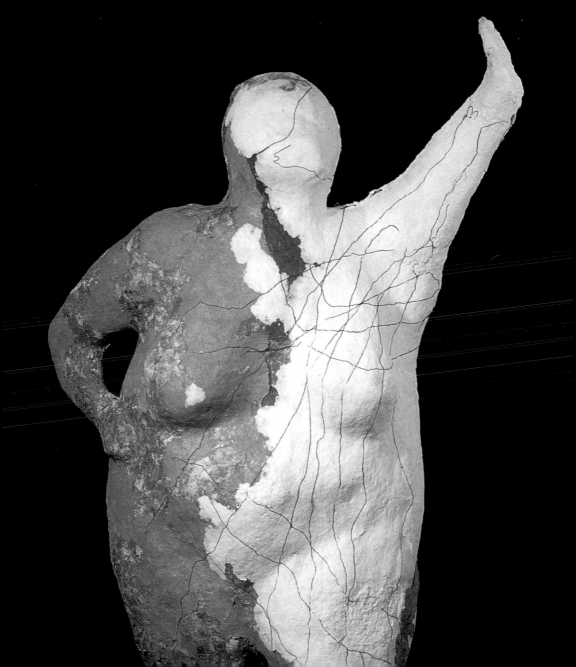

Helmut Becker was born in Canada and educated there, as well as in the United States, and the Netherlands. He is now Professor Emeritus at the University of Western Ontario, in London, Canada. He has been making paper and studying the form the fibers can take for many years. He has a particular interest is the development of alternatives to trees as a source for papermaking, and recently has taken part in studies and experiments into the use of hemp; the "industrial" *Cannabis sative* (low THC level— the active principle of cannabis). In his search for the highest-quality materials, Becker not only grows his own raw materials but is now preparing his own natural colorings, importing his own supply of lapis lazuli from Argentina for that purpose.

Sativa Sun Kite
Hemp ribbons 4ft (122cm) diameter
Helmut Becker 1998

MANY OF MY RECENT HANDMADE PAPER/SCULPTURE ART WORKS HAVE RELATED TO TREES AND THE SURVIVAL OF TREES AND OUR ENVIRONMENT. TO SLOW DOWN OR STOP THE GIGANTIC CONSUMPTION OF TREES FOR THE MASS PRODUCTION OF PAPER PULP, GROWING HEMP PLANTS FOR PAPER IS ONE VIABLE ALTERNATIVE. THE GESTURE OF THE *SATIVA SUN KITE* IS ONE OF HOPE.

NEAL BONHAM

Neal Bonham first discovered handmade paper when he was at the University of Wisconsin in the early 1970s. Following this, he and his wife, Suzanne Ferris, moved to Seattle where they set up their private press and paper mill making paper for fine letterpress printing. Neal was able to cultivate his interest in watermarks and developed the technique that he now uses to create works of art. Suzanne creates the original drawings that are then transferred onto sheets of polyurethane foam and impressed into the surface using a heated tool. The pieces of foam then become the basis of the paper mold and fine colored pulp is used to build up the image. Once the image is complete, it is couched with a strong backing layer.

Agave Parryi
12in x 10in (30cm x 25cm)
Neal Bonham 1995

I HAVE A SENTIMENTAL ATTACHMENT TO THE SUSPENSION OF FIBERS IN WATER BECAUSE THAT IS WHAT PAPERMAKING IS—A NATURAL DEPOSIT OF FIBERS ON A MOLD. I MAKE IMAGES BY GUIDING THE FIBER FLOW INDIRECTLY.

INGER-JOHANNE BRAUTASET
After studying tapestry at the National College of Arts and Crafts in Oslo, Norwegian Inger-Johanne Brautaset spent more than 20 years weaving tapestries for architectural projects. Then, in 1987, she first discovered the art of working with paper during a year spent at the West Norway Academy of Art in Bergen. Her artistic expression is communicated through compressed paper sheets—imprinted with the uneven, frayed, and torn edges characteristic of pulp—which are built into precise, concrete, sculptural forms. By creating forms with layers of pulp, Brautaset works against the concept of paper as merely a neutral supporting surface.

Strata Rust
5¾ft x 4¾ft x 17½in
(1.75m x 1.45m x 45cm)
Inger-Johanne Brautaset 1991

TRYING TO DEFINE YOUR IDENTITY IN A CONTEMPORARY WORLD THAT IS UNDERGOING CONTINUAL AND DRAMATIC CHANGES, YOU REALIZE THAT YOU ARE YOURSELF A PRODUCT OF HISTORY. TRACES OF OUR PREDECESSORS SUCH AS ROCK CARVINGS AND BEAUTIFUL TOOLS PASS ON THEIR ARTISTIC MESSAGE ACROSS THE AGES LIKE SIGNALS TO BE RECEIVED AND DECIPHERED. SCULPTURES BUILT FROM A HUNDRED SHEETS OF PAPER CAN BE THE ARTIST'S INTERPRETATION OF STRATA OF ANCIENT CIVILIZATIONS REVEALED IN AN ARCHAEOLOGICAL SITE.

KATHRYN CLARK

Studying printmaking at Wittenberg University and at Wayne State University, both in the United States, gave Kathryn Clark her love of paper and an understanding that it is more than just the vehicle on which the artist places an image. Early inspiration came from medieval and Oriental manuscripts and book illustrations. Clark works with layers of incredibly fine, thin skims of paper made from very dilute pulp. Fine threads are sometimes added to represent lines of type and some pieces are embellished with folded structures to look like a pop-up book. The whole keeps the viewer constantly aware of the relationship between the plain sheet of paper and what it can become and express.

Which comes first, the book or the page?
34in x 48in (86cm x 122cm)
Kathryn Clark 1983

EACH MEDIUM GIVES THE ARTIST A DIFFERENT AESTHETIC TOOL WITH WHICH TO CREATE PERSONAL IMAGERY. IT IS IMPORTANT TO CONSIDER AND UNDERSTAND THE PHYSICAL CHARACTERISTICS OF PAPER PULP WHEN CREATING MATERIAL WITH IT, JUST AS AN ARTIST SHOULD WITH ANY MATERIAL. UNLIKE ALMOST ANY OTHER MEDIUM, HOWEVER, PAPER PULP CAN INTEGRATE AND COMBINE OTHER MATERIALS SUCH AS INK, PAINT, PENCIL, AND PASTELS.

KATE COOLAHAN

Kate Coolahan's work is all about the structures that surround us, and it discusses a variety of issues. The piece shown here is the first of a series called *Winged Victories and Clipped Wings*, in which the pieces represent the strong yet sometimes inadequate and frustrating structures with which women have had to wrestle—sometimes succeeding, at other times not. Coolahan's work is influenced by the climate of her native New Zealand, evoking the wind and the sun, which falls on an unprotected land through the holes in the ozone layer. Her work is frequently presented in beautifully made boxes, which allow her to get over the difficulty of moving three-dimensional pieces over long distances.

Winged Victories and Clipped Wings
16½in x 41½in x 6½in
(42cm x 106cm x 16cm)
Kate Coolahan 1992/1997

WINGED VICTORIES AND CLIPPED WINGS IS A PAINTED BACKGROUND, A STORM AT SEA, WITH XEROXES SUN-BLEACHED FROM SOLAR RADIATION. AESTHETICALLY, NOTHING CAN MATCH THE RANGE OF FEELING THAT PAPER CAN COMMUNICATE.

KATHY CRUMP

Artist Kathy Crump now lives in California, but following her art education in Oregon, Connecticut, and California she traveled widely to lecture in Australia and Europe, as well as the United States. Her work is found in a number of locations in the United States, Europe, and Japan. She has also written extensively on the various aspects of the craft of papermaking, discussing the different plants that can be used, including suitable dye plants. Crump's work, which is normally quite large, deals with issues of permanence and fragility in all our lives, with destruction and regeneration, with communication through both the written and printed word.

Paper Journey

Reynolds Gallery,
University of the Pacific, California.
25ft x 22in (7.6m x 56cm)

Kathy Crump 1996

"PAPER JOURNEY TRACES WRITING FROM BEFORE CHRIST TO COMPUTER LANGUAGE. PAPER HAS BEEN AN INTEGRAL PART OF THIS JOURNEY IN SOME CULTURES FROM AS EARLY AS 200 BCE.**"**

JEAN DAVEY-WINTER

When Jean Davey-Winter went to Birmingham College of Art and Design in England, she studied textiles, and these have always been an important part of her life as an artist. Textiles are made of fibers, and those fibers, broken down, are re-formed into paper. Gradually these two areas of interest mingled so that, by 1991, she was also interested in printmaking. A visit to Mexico inspired works based on ancient pre-Hispanic Mexican cosmology. The main material used for the two-dimensional piece shown here is recycled paper that is made up of many layers, poured rather than dipped, then embossed with traces of pre-Hispanic carved imagery relating to the ancient pyramids and palaces. Finally, the surface was waxed and colored with paints and pigments.

Omeyocan II
4½ft x 6ft (1.4m x 1.8m)
Jean Davey-Winter 1989

OMEYOCAN II FORMED PART OF A SERIES OF PAPER WORKS THAT WERE PRODUCED FOLLOWING A VISIT TO MEXICO. PRE-HISPANIC MEXICAN COSMOLOGY IS BOTH FASCINATING AND COMPLEX—OMEYOCAN IS THE "PLACE OF DUALITY," THE THIRTEENTH SKY, FROM WHERE LIFE EMANATED WITH ITS TWO FACES AND ITS TWO OPPOSING FORCES.

AMANDA DEGENER

The winter landscape of Minnesota and the trees she observes when cross-country skiing are the inspiration for Amanda Degener's pieces. Her current work is made from *kozo* and *gampi* fibers imported from Japan and Taiwan and cooked, beaten, and formed into individual sheets in her workshop. Each piece is separately colored, painted, dyed, or stained, using only natural materials such as walnut stain or red and black iron oxide. Her work often includes recycled paper in an effort to encourage the use of discarded materials. Most of Amanda Degener's influences have come from the area around her home in Minnesota, but she has spent time in Italy and has exhibited in Korea and Japan as well as extensively in the United States.

Inner Bark, Inner Light
17½ft x 5ft (5.33m x 1.5m) diameter
Amanda Degener 1992

I MAKE PAPER BECAUSE I AM OBSESSIVELY ADDICTED TO THE PROCESS AND I CAN PAY ATTENTION TO THE RELATIONSHIP BETWEEN THE COLOR, TEXTURE, AND THICKNESS OF EACH SHEET. ONCE THE PAPER IS IN THE DRY STAGE, I OFTEN DRAW OR PAINT ON IT WITH NATURAL DYES, SUMI INK, BEESWAX, AND OXIDES.

INGE EVERS

Inge Evers works mostly in her studio in Haarlem, the Netherlands, but has traveled widely to study papermaking in the United States and Japan. Her interest in paper is intertwined with a fascination with the structures of felt—both are nonwoven materials with great similarities in the way they are made. She spent several months with feltmakers in Moscow and Turkmenistan and traveled through the deserts of central Asia into Uzbekistan, a route that almost reverses the passage of the knowledge of papermaking from China to the West. Evers also works as an art therapist encouraging students to consider the process of making both felt and paper as a way of learning about art and as an artistic way of healing through making things, performance, ritual, and celebration.

Food for the Soul
Handmade silk paper, combined with paper rope and Japanese *kozo* paper
5¼ft (160cm) almost circular

Inge Evers 1998

PAPER TRANSCENDENT

IN FRONT OF LATE SUNSET

SHE WHO IS CALLED SWEET SUN

ILLUMINATES TRANSPARENCY

SPARKLING LIGHT OUTLINES

POINTING PYRAMID SHADOW

CAROL FARROW

Carol Farrow has a home in London, as well as a studio in France, where she works with ceramics as well as paper. Her work is influenced by architectural surfaces and objects bearing the marks of use, implying the passage of time and change. She is enthused by paper that in its wet state can be cast or molded to form any texture, thickness, shape, size, color, or degree of porosity. For Farrow the process of working with paper can be simple or complex, but the basic operation of forming paper from fibers— separate elements that come together to form a structure—is fundamental to her working in the medium. Her works are formed from cotton fibers, beaten in water and then made into sheets. These are then pressed, dried, painted, and often impregnated with wax.

Ancienne (diptych)
Patterned form created by casting cotton linters onto wood
6⅞ft x 4½ft (2.06m x 1.32m)
Carol Farrow 1989

I TRY TO EXTRACT THE RICH QUALITIES OF THINGS WORN, DETERIORATED, OR AFFECTED BY AGE TO CREATE IMAGES EMBODYING A HISTORY OF DECAY AND RENEWAL. THE PROCESS I USE ALLOWS FOR MANIPULATION AND CONTROL AT EVERY STAGE BUT, MOST IMPORTANTLY, IT INVITES CHANGE AND TRANSFORMATION.

BETTY FRIEDMAN

The work of this artist combines the skills and demands of both printmaking and papermaking. At her studio in Oakland, California, she makes sheets of paper in the Western manner on a traditional laid mold, but she uses a diversity of materials, including the Oriental *kozo*. Sheets are formed in a variety of weights and colored with powdered pigments, as well as with natural dyes. Some of the sheets are fine and delicate for use in the process known as *chine a colle*, in which paper is layered before being passed through the etching press to unite the layers. Additional layers and colors can then be added and the sheet pressed again. As well as making the paper that forms the basis of her own art, Friedman is commissioned to make sheets for other artists.

Untitled 107
19½in x 26in (50cm x 66cm)
Betty Friedman

EACH PRINT IS A ONE-OFF IMAGE, NOT PART OF AN EDITION. WITH ONLY ONE CHANCE TO PRINT CORRECTLY, I TRY TO PREDICT THE OUTCOME BY USING REGISTRATION, OVERLAYS, AND DRAW-DOWNS, OR INK COLOR TESTS, TO GET SOME IDEA OF HOW THE FINISHED PIECE WILL LOOK. THERE IS ALWAYS A RANDOM, UNCONTROLLED SURPRISE ELEMENT WHEN I PULL THE PRINT.

PAT GENTENAAR-TORLEY

Pat Gentenaar-Torley completed her arts education in the fiber arts department of the California College of Arts and Crafts in Oakland, where she discovered papermaking. Now working in the Netherlands, she has developed a technique she refers to as pulp painting, in which the color mostly comes from the natural tones of the various plant materials she works with. Her works are made up of layers of different-colored and different-textured pulps which are carefully poured and added to the piece on a vacuum table, which helps remove excess water. A final layer of hemp pulp is added to connect all parts of the surface image. Each fiber reflects the light in a different way, according to its individual texture, and this quality gives the piece a rich surface quality that cannot be duplicated in any other medium.

Golden Glow
21in x 25½in (53cm x 65cm)
Pat Gentenaar-Torley 1998

ALTHOUGH THE PAPER/PLANT FIBERS ARE NO LONGER GROWING, THEY RETAIN THEIR STRUCTURAL ABILITY TO REACT TO THEIR SURROUNDINGS. NO LONGER SOARING INTO THE AIR, THEY ARE NEVERTHELESS STILL PART OF LIFE. SEE HOW THE FIBERS CREATE THE SURFACES, UNDULATING AND PULLING. SEE HOW THE LIFE THAT CREATED THE FIBERS GIVES THEM FORM, EVEN NOW.

PETER GENTENAAR

Before gaining his Masters in printmaking at the California College of Arts and Crafts in Oakland, Peter Gentenaar studied fine art in the Netherlands and Italy. Later, he undertook a week-long study visit to a paper mill in the Netherlands, where he learned the basics of papermaking. From here Gentenaar was ready to develop his own ideas. For his work he beats long fibers of hemp and flax for as long as possible so that each one absorbs the maximum amount of water. Once the sheets have been formed into an art work they are allowed to dry naturally and the enormous loss of water from the fibers causes the piece to shrink and contort. Although there is some control over this, the artist is always surprised at just how much smaller and more intense the forms have become.

Light Object
7ft x 5½ft (2.1m x 1.7m)
Peter Gentenaar 1996

WELL-BEATEN LINEN SHRINKS AND, AS IT STRETCHES BETWEEN STIFF COUNTERPARTS, CAN BE PLAYED LIKE A DRUM. WATER HAS AGAIN GIVEN FORM TO FIBERS THAT WERE ONCE THE BACKBONE OF VEGETATION. ALMOST MAGICALLY, GENETIC CODES ARE MADE VISIBLE. OPAQUE AND TRANSPARENT FORMS EMBRACE THE LIGHT THAT FALLS ON—AND SOMETIMES PENETRATES—THE LINEN-MADE PAPER.

HELEN HIEBERT

Helen Hiebert is based in Portland, Oregon, but she learned papermaking at Dieu Donné Paper Mill in New York, where she also worked for a number of years. Dieu Donné is famous not only for its artistic craftsmanship, but also for beautiful handmade sheets of paper. Hiebert specializes in sculptural pieces, mostly in the form of lamps, which, when illuminated, show the design created within each sheet of paper. Watermark images are made by layering material on the paper mold so that the pulp is thinly spread in these areas, forming an image to be released by light. Although she uses mostly cotton and abaca fibers—from a plant related to the banana—she has extensive knowledge of other materials. In common with many other artists, Hiebert passes on her knowledge by teaching.

Bloom: Yellow petals over a steel armature

30in x 24in x 24in
(76cm x 61cm x 61cm)

Helen Hiebert 1998

I AM FASCINATED BY LIGHT AND I MANIPULATE PAPER BY CUTTING, LAYERING, WEAVING, AND CREATING WATERMARKS IN HANDMADE PAPERS TO PRODUCE CREATIVE LIGHTING OBJECTS WHICH EXPLORE THE INTERACTION OF PAPER AND LIGHT. THE FORM MY SHADES TAKE IS CREATED DURING THE PAPERMAKING PROCESS. I USE A VARIETY OF PAPERMAKING TECHNIQUES, SUCH AS EMBEDDING WIRE IN SHEETS OF WET PAPER TO CREATE STRUCTURE.

KYOKO IBE

Kyoko Ibe was educated in Kyoto, Japan's old capital and the center for the history of the country's artistic heritage. Ibe absorbed the culture of her past, understanding the important part that *washi* had played. This fine handmade paper was used for all types of practical purposes as well as the means of creating works of art—but it had not been observed as a work of art itself. Ibe realized what an enormous amount she could express by using the medium as itself. She has taken waste material, newspapers, old exercise books, and waste computer paper and refashioned it into sculptural installations, which make the viewer aware of space, light, movement, and form. Some of the installations Ibe has created are on a truly monumental scale.

Habataku–94
Silk paper
957sq yd x 82ft (800sq m x 25m)
Kyoko Ibe 1994

"THE SHEETS I MAKE ARE NOT "PAPER," THEY HAVE TO BE WORKS OF ART. AS SUCH, I DO NOT DO ANYTHING OTHER THAN HAVING MY WORK REFLECT THE INTRINSIC MERITS AND SPECIAL PROPERTIES OF THE MATERIAL DIRECTLY. IT DOESN'T WORK THROUGH THE FORM OF "PAPER.""

EIJA ISOJÄRVI

The work of Finnish artist Eija Isojärvi is both two- and three-dimensional and can be found in collections in Scandinavia, the Netherlands, and Germany. She has also exhibited in the United States, showing her work in New York at Dieu Donné and in Chicago at the Schaumburg Art Museum. Linen is the predominant raw material for Isojärvi's paper work, but she also uses other materials, including cotton. Her work is in the form of large two-dimensional reliefs, big sculptural objects, such as the one shown here, or installations.

Drawings
18ft x 5ft (55½m x 15½m)
Eija Isojärvi 1996

ONE IMAGE HAS ACCOMPANIED ME THROUGH TIME. IT WAS IN MY HEART BEFORE I WAS BORN. THIS IMAGE CHANGES AS MY LIFE CHANGES AND EXPRESSES ITSELF IN NEW FORMS AND COLORS. I CANNOT LEAVE IT OR SEPARATE FROM IT. IT IS A VISION OF THE WORLD AND SPACE AS UNITY, AN IMAGE THAT MAKES ME UNDERSTAND SOMETHING ABOUT MYSELF.

EEVA-LIISA ISOMAA

Having trained and worked as a printmaker in Finland, Eeva-Liisa Isomaa has developed an interest in papermaking as a way of expressing her experience and her feeling for strong, natural landscapes. This art frequently takes the form of graphic books, which she has been making for the last four or five years. These take different forms and dimensions; they may be fine and delicate, transparent books with handmade linen pages, or larger books making bolder statements, or, as here, an installation of books forming a waterfall on the wall. A visit to Iceland in 1997 was particularly inspirational.

Cascade
22 books, various sizes
Eeva-Liisa Isomaa 1998

AS A GRAPHIC ARTIST I HAVE A CLOSE RELATIONSHIP WITH PAPER. PAPER IS NOT JUST SOME BACKGROUND TO THE WORK—IT IS PART OF THE WORK ITSELF. I USE SOME PAPER FOR ITS TRANSPARENCY, SOME BECAUSE OF ITS STRUCTURE; WHITE LINEN PAPER IS LIKE TRANSPARENT ICE, BROWN LINEN IS LIKE SKIN—THE PAPER ITSELF HAS A STRONG CHARACTER.

JOANNA KESSEL

After studying in Edinburgh and at the Royal College of Art in London, Joanna Kessel spent a year in Barcelona, in contact with other papermakers and with the Paper Museum at Cappellades. Since moving to West Yorkshire in 1994, her work has been greatly influenced by the surrounding landscape. The piece featured here, *Book: Earth*, is a study of England's longest footpath, the Pennine Way. Kessel sieved earth samples from 15 different locations along the route and incorporated them in sheets of handmade paper, formed in the traditional way from cotton and linen. The sheets were then protected by a coating of wax before being mounted as leaves from an unbound book pinned to a beam of ancient oak.

Book: Earth

35in x 9in x 4½in
(89cm x 23cm x 12cm)

Joanna Kessel 1996

THE WORK LOOSELY TAKES THE FORM OF A BOOK AND BECOMES A MEANS OF RECORDING THE LANDSCAPE. EACH SET OF LEAVES REPRESENTS A SPECIFIC PLACE ALONG A STRETCH OF THE PENNINE WAY. COLOR IS DERIVED FROM THE PIGMENTATION IN THE SOIL SAMPLES GATHERED AT EACH LOCATION. ALTHOUGH SUBTLE, THE COLOR VARIATION IS EASILY VISIBLE AND INSTILLS A SENSE OF PLACE AND MATERIAL.

NAOMI KOBAYASHI

Japan is a country of fine textiles and fine handmade paper, or *washi*. At university in Tokyo, Naomi Kobayashi studied both textiles and papermaking and she has continued to make works of art in both media. Her work is housed in collections in Japan, Europe, Israel, Mexico, and the United States. She has exhibited in all these countries as well as in Turkey, another country renowned for its textiles. Writing about her approach to her preferred medium, she describes going for a walk early one morning and observing the dew spangles on fine spiders' webs and the newly risen sun imparting a silvery sparkle to the rice paddies. This made her acutely aware of herself as part of nature's changing pattern, and her work reflects her wish to depict the cycles of life and the eternal cycles of the universe.

Cosmic Ring N5
7½ft x 7½ft x 8in
(2.3m x 2.3m x 20cm)
Naomi Kobayashi 1996

I BECAME INCREASINGLY AWARE OF THE RELATIONSHIP BETWEEN MY WORK AND THE SPACE SURROUNDING IT. THIS LED ME TO WANT TO CREATE AN ART THAT WAS TRANSPARENT ENOUGH TO ALLOW WIND AND LIGHT TO PASS THROUGH IT. I HAVE BEEN EXPLORING FORMS THAT ARE AS LIGHT AND FREE AS THE AIR. AS A RESULT, THE INTENTION OF MY MORE RECENT WORK IS TO COMMUNICATE THE UNITY OF NATURE'S CONTINUAL PROVIDENCE.

HARRI LEPPÄNEN

As both sculptor and printmaker, Harri Leppänen makes and uses paper to create the images he desires. He beats linen in his Hollander then forms the sheets of handmade paper that will be used, while still wet, to mold a sculpture. The piece is then allowed to dry out slowly before being patinated and gilded, after which it is sealed, usually with wax, to protect it. For his two-dimensional pieces, Leppänen protects, or seals, certain parts of the sheet by gilding or waxing and applies an image to the rest of the surface using offset lithography. The artist has exhibited widely and his work is well represented in many public collections in his native Finland.

Prisoner of His Own Life
Linen fiber, gilding metal
5½ft x 15¾in x 15¾in
(170cm x 40cm x 40cm)

Harri Leppänen 1998

MAKING SCULPTURES IS, FOR ME, AN ESCAPE FROM THE STEP-BY-STEP PROCESS OF GRAPHIC ART. SCULPTURES EVOLVE, UNPLANNED, ONE OUT OF THE OTHER—OLD WORKS GIVE BIRTH TO NEW ONES, NOT ONLY LENDING THE IDEAS, BUT ALSO PART OF THE STRUCTURE: A NEW SCULPTURE MAY CONTAIN PARTS OF OLDER WORKS.

GÉZA MÉSZÁROS

Géza Mészáros was born in Budapest, Hungary, where he studied fine art. He then went on to specialize in the skill of fresco painting, working with the exponent of the art Aurel Bernath. By 1981, however, his interest had shifted to the artistic possibilities afforded by paper and he was able to set up his studio at the Paper Mill Budafok. Mészáros' interest in paper as an art medium in its own right developed rapidly and in 1986 he became a founder member of IAPMA (International Association of Papermakers and Paper Artists), a highly respected organization of which he was to become an Honorary Life Member ten years later. Like other paper artists, he also has an interest in textiles and has previously taken part in an exhibition of Hungarian handmade tapestry held in Berlin.

The Colors of Water
24½in x 25in (62cm x 63cm)
Géza Mészáros 1997

I AM INCLINED TO THINK THAT THE PRESENT, THE LIVABLE MOMENTS OF PRESENT, ARE THE ENDLESS INTERSECTING PLANES OF AN UNRECOGNIZABLE DEPTH. PRESENT TIME IS THE ONLY DIMENSION. MY GILDED, SHAPED, AND PAINTED WORKS ARE TO ME GIFTS OF THE MOST ANCIENT RITE, PAINTING. THEY ARE TRULY LIVED MOMENTS OF MY EXISTENCE.

REBECCA MILNER

Books can be "read" in a variety of ways. With the piece shown here, Rebecca Milner, who studied graphic design and illustration before earning her Masters degree in Book Arts at the Camberwell School of Art in London, uses the form to make the viewer "read" a "shape." *Migration* is about the predestination of behavior. Wildebeest have to travel to find food and water and *Migration* reveals the preordained plan— the books show the map lines depicting the routes of the animals, just as the veins in the animals' bodies carry the message that impels them to act. The form of the piece gives the moving shape of the herd; the structure of each book evokes each animal. The piece as a whole provokes the viewer to think about how much of human behavior is preplanned.

Migration

500 handmade books of Fabriano
Ingres paper, sewn on raised cords
with linen thread
16sq ft (1.5sq m)
Rebecca Milner 1998

IN THE WORK I HAVE ADAPTED THE ROLE OF THE BOOK, WHICH HAS TRADITIONALLY SOUGHT TO ENLIGHTEN READERS, TO SYMBOLIZE THE INSTINCTIVE KNOWLEDGE HELD BY WILDEBEEST. IT IS THIS KNOWLEDGE WHICH ENABLES THEM TO MAKE THEIR JOURNEYS GENERATION AFTER GENERATION, KNOWLEDGE WHICH IS INACCESSIBLE TO HUMANS.

CATHERINE NASH

Catherine Nash grew up near the water's edge in New England, practically raised on a sailing boat by her sea-loving father. She gained a degree in fine art from the University of New Hampshire and then went on to study for a Masters at the University of Arizona. She still lives in Arizona—the ocean of her childhood has been replaced by the ocean of the desert. In 1987, after a year in Europe studying printmaking, she spent several months in Japan learning about handmaking paper and woodblock printing. Nash now creates three-dimensional works—shelters, sanctuaries, caves—drawing her inspiration from the forts she built as a child growing up in the woods of New England. Her paper vessels are formed using Japanese and Nepalese techniques, to create strong sheets that are thin and three-dimensional.

Ancient Ocean—Nesting Boats
8ft x 4½ft x 3ft (2.5m x 1.4m x 0.9m)
Catherine Nash 1997

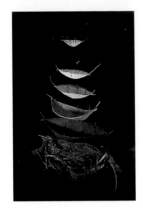

THE BOATS WE CHOOSE TO JOURNEY IN CAN EVOLVE IN SHAPE AND SIZE AND PURPOSE. ONE BEGETS ANOTHER. EACH SUCCESSIVE VESSEL CAN BECOME MORE BEAUTIFUL, MORE REFINED. THE BOAT IS THE SYMBOL OF OUR JOURNEY THROUGH TIME AND SPACE, AN EPHEMERAL "SKIN" CONJURING UP THE BOUNDARY OF OUR BEING.

JULIE NORRIS

While Julie Norris was at the Warrington College of Art in England she became inspired by handmade paper, having seen a sheet of handmade watercolor paper from the Barcham Green Mill in Kent. After finishing her degree at Liverpool Polytechnic, she went on to the environmental media department at The Royal College of Art in London to continue her study of papermaking and to develop her understanding of its possibilities as an artistic medium. This led Norris to discover Japanese papers, and today most of her work is created from repulped *gampi* tissue which she uses to create subtle cast forms.

Whitby
37in x 29in (94cm x 74cm)
Julie Norris 1988

A COLLAGE OF NEWSPAPER, BANDAGES, STRING, AND AN OLD CREPE SCARF WAS COVERED IN RECYCLED *GAMPI* PULP. WHEN DRY, MOST OF THESE ITEMS WERE REMOVED. THE SCARF LEFT TRACES OF DYE AND SEQUINS. PASTEL DRAWINGS WERE ADDED TO THE NEWSPAPER.

JACKI PARRY

Jacki Parry was born in Australia and studied art in Melbourne, where her primary interest was sculpture. Following her move to the United Kingdom, she based herself in Glasgow, first studying and then teaching, and became a founder of The Paper Workshop. Her work has been extensively exhibited in the United Kingdom, Europe, Australia, and Japan and can be found in many public collections. Parry continues to investigate the ways in which paper behaves, both as substrate and in combination with other materials. Her major interest is in the structural aspects of the pulp itself and in a paper membrane that is both strong and translucent. She is constantly researching new fibers to discover their potential.

Ways of Editing

Cast handmade paper
7¾in x 7½in x 2in
(19.5cm x 19cm x 5cm)

Jacki Parry 1998

PAPER IS THE MOST COMMON SUBSTRATE FOR THE CARRYING OF INFORMATION. THESE OBJECTS ARE PART OF A LARGER BODY OF DIVERSE WORKS IN TWO AND THREE DIMENSIONS ENTITLED *WAYS OF EDITING*. IN THIS GROUP, CULTURAL ARTIFACTS ARE REFERENCED TO EXPLORE WAYS IN WHICH "INFORMATION" IS CREATED AND EDITED, EXPOSED AND CONCEALED.

JANE PONSFORD

Jane Ponsford's use of paper is almost sculptural. She describes her work as being concerned with accumulating cast paper fragments into an ordered structure. The formal qualities of the piece are her prime interest at first, but later the way small elements catch the light becomes important. She works mostly with cotton linters. If they are left white they give a pure look to the piece; if colored, a clear tone. The pulp is dyed in the vat, then small sheets are formed in 6in by 3in (15cm by 7.5cm) molds improvised from car body repair mesh. Each sheet is then cast onto a slightly larger scrap of fabric and folded over before an initial pressing to remove excess water. Each little parcel is then carefully unwrapped and dried. Later any wires or threads incorporated into the sheets are joined to form the overall structure.

Color Field (blue)

Cast paper pulp, dye, wire and nylon thread
5¼ft x 10in (160cm x 26cm)

Jane Ponsford 1997

I COME FROM A BACKGROUND IN PAINTING BUT HAVE ALWAYS BEEN ATTRACTED TO SCULPTURE AND MAKING THINGS. WORKING WITH PAPER AS I DO IS LIKE THE MIDWAY POINT BETWEEN THE TWO. THE FREEDOM OF CASTING PAPER IS TEMPERED BY THE FORMALITY OF THE STRUCTURE OF WIRE AND THREADS.

DOROTHEA REESE-HEIM

Dorothea Reese-Heim studied at
the Academy of Fine Art,
Karlsruhre and also in Munich,
where she developed an interest
in textiles. In 1981 she came under
the influence of Eduardo Paolozzi,
when the specially commissioned
paper studio and workshop was
opened in Munich, studying the
basic structures that can be formed
from this material. Dr. Reese-Heim
makes her sheets from hemp and
kozo and other available
vegetable fiber, as well as recycled
cotton and linen fabric. She is one
of the founding members of IAPMA
(International Association of
Papermakers and Paper Artists),
which was formed in 1986 at
Düren at the Leopold Hoesch
Museum during the Biennale
der Papierkunst.

Gesprengte Bögen
5¼ft x 5¼ft x 3¼ft (1.6m x 1.6m x 1m)
Dorothea Reese-Heim 1992/98

THE UNDERLYING LANGUAGE IS THAT OF THE CIRCLE IN ITS MOVEMENT, THE CRESCENT, BUT ALSO THE VICTOR'S LAUREL AND FUNERAL WREATH. AS SHELLS THE SHEETS ARE BOTH PROTECTIVE AND DISMISSIVE, AS CURVES THEY SHOW FLEETING TRIUMPH AND AS A CRESCENT THEY REPRESENT A SYMBOL OF VANITY. THERE ALSO EMERGES THE IMPRESSION OF DOUBLING UP IN PAIN AND OPEN WOUNDS, OF REARING UP AND COLLAPSE, VICTORY AND DEFEAT, JOY AND SORROW.

MAUREEN RICHARDSON

Maureen Richardson came to papermaking after many years of work in other areas of craftsmanship, in particular rush-and-straw work and basketry and woodcarving. This led her to take a course in papermaking at the Camberwell School of Art in London. She soon discovered that her inspiration came from the variety of plants that could be used to form sheets of paper—rush, straw, bracken, and brassica were regularly used to create sheets of textured paper. As a result of her friendship with Dr. Ragab of the Cairo Institute of Papyrus, she began to create beautiful artworks in what she terms vegetable papyrus. Her work has inspired a degree of experimentation with a material which many would not have contemplated using for paper-based objects even a few years ago.

Kiwi Fruit Papyrus Bowl
10in x 4in x 4in (25cm x 10cm x 10cm)
Maureen Richardson 1996

IF THERE IS A BOUNDARY BETWEEN PAPERMAKING AS A CRAFT PROCESS AND PAPER ART, I HAVE SOMEHOW DRIFTED ACROSS IT WITHOUT ANY CONSCIOUS INTENTION. WHILE IT IS POSSIBLE TO WRITE INTELLIGIBLY ABOUT HOW PAPER IS MADE, I DO NOT PERSONALLY BELIEVE THAT IT IS USEFUL TO TRY AND EXPLAIN IN WORDS THE MEANING OF A WORK OF ART. IT IS ENOUGH FOR ME TO DECLARE MY DELIGHT IN MAKING IT.

PRISCILLA ROBINSON

After attending art school in Washington, DC, New York, and Tucson, Arizona, Priscilla Robinson began painting canvases dealing with textures floating in space. Then, in about 1983, a friend showed her how to make paper, giving her the opportunity to express shape, color, texture, shadow, and space through the materials themselves. She works mostly with abaca and cotton fibers and in recent work Robinson has concentrated on triangular shapes. Pulp is cast into the required shapes on felts, which may already have textures applied to them. Excess water is then removed by means of a vacuum pump and the shapes are colored and decorated with acrylic paints, gold leaf, or beads.

24 Butterflies
17in x 39in x 3in (43cm x 99cm x 7.5cm)
Priscilla Robinson 1997

THE PROCESS OF MAKING PAPER IS A WAY TO BRING THE OUTSIDE INSIDE. BY TAKING PLANT FIBERS AND ALTERING THEM, I CAN STAY CLOSE TO THE NATURAL WAY OF THINGS. I HELP THE FIBERS DO WHAT THEY WANT TO DO AND, IN LISTENING TO THEIR SILENT MESSAGES, I FEEL MORE A PART OF THE UNIVERSE.

FRED SIEGENTHALER

Fred Siegenthaler was among the first artists in Europe to start making paper works. After his apprenticeship at the Biberist Paper Mill, he furthered his studies in Munich as a paper engineer, and then at the Basel School of Art and Design in Switzerland, where he learned the skills of woodcutting. Three years' travel in Thailand gave him an extensive knowledge of Oriental papermaking methods. Siegenthaler's own initial papermaking experimented with such unconventional materials as leather waste, plastic, hay, tobacco, and abandoned wasps' nests. From 1967, he was commissioned to produce papers for other artists including Robert Rauschenberg, Tatyana Grosman, Lary Rivers, Marc Chagall, and Joan Miró. Today, Siegenthaler creates only his own works of art.

Don't Leave Me
Paper relief, linen fibers
24in x 20in (60cm x 50cm)
Fred Siegenthaler 1992

NOTWITHSTANDING ALL INNOVATIONS AND EXPERIMENTS, SIEGENTHALER'S WORKS ARE NOT DOMINATED BY HIS CRAFT, OR HIS MATERIAL; RATHER, WITH PAPER AND PAPER FIBER AS MATERIAL, HE HAS COMPOSED THESE WORKS OF ART INTO A CONVINCING PERSONAL STATEMENT.

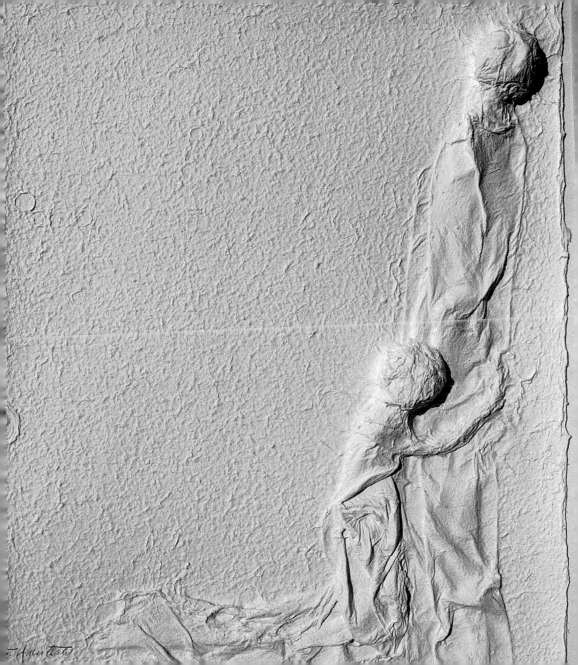

ROBBIN AMI SILVERBERG

Since about 1983 Robbin Ami Silverberg has been involved in paper works. Following her degree in art history and sculpture, she spent three years working in Austria as a book artist and paper designer, which naturally resulted in a greater involvement with paper as art. Her art takes the form of small edition artist's books and large paper installations. Her work has been widely exhibited in the United States and also in Hungary. The scrolls featured here show how watermarks are used to represent "writings" within the sheet of paper, allowing light to pass through and reflect off objects embedded in their surfaces. She has published and lectured widely and her work is found in public collections in the United States, Canada, South Africa, Germany, and Hungary.

Scrolls (eggshell, tea, and mica)
Each 30ft x 2ft (9m x 60cm)
Robbin Ami Silverberg 1995/96

I APPROACH THE ARTIST'S BOOK AS A COMPLEX CONTAINER OF INFORMATION. PAPER DOMINATES BOTH MY ARTIST'S BOOKS AND INSTALLATIONS AS A METAPHOR FOR SKIN, THE PROTECTIVE YET FRAGILE SURFACE OF THE HUMAN BODY. THESE SURFACES HAVE RESONANCE AND TRANSLUCENCY, ALLOWING FOR A MULTIPLE SENSORY EXPERIENCE.

MARIAN SMIT

Marian Smit trained as a teacher and gave lessons in many areas of craftsmanship, including needlework of various kinds. She progressed to weaving and knitting, and then papermaking, which she began in 1991. Her move to the island of Texel in the North Sea in 1994 increased the influences of natural phenomena on her work. With her studio based at the foot of a lighthouse—the symbol of safety—the effects of the elements on human life became ever more apparent. Smit makes small pieces of paper, which she colors in the vat. They are joined together, often with copper wire, and may be flat or rolled, gradually building up a collage inspired by the elements.

Flying Impossible 1
Wire, paper, and sheet
8in x 6in x 6in (20cm x 15cm x 15cm)
Marian Smit 1997

I MAKE SMALL ELEMENTS, WHICH I JOIN TOGETHER TO FORM A LARGER ONE. SMALL PIECES OF PAPER BECOME A BIGGER STRUCTURE. AT THE MOMENT I WORK WITH COPPER WIRE BOUND IN PAPER. ALMOST ALWAYS IT IS NATURE THAT IS MY INSPIRATION.

KAREN STAHLECKER

Karen Stahlecker gained her Masters in fine art and sculpture at the School of Art Institute in Chicago and followed this up with a far-reaching study of handmaking paper in Europe and Japan. This knowledge of Western and Oriental traditions is now evident in her work. According to the requirements of a particular piece, she will either make sheets out of *kozo* or *gampi*—to obtain fine translucent sheets—or she will employ the European tradition and use cotton or linen. The finished sheets, sometimes colored, are then laminated to armatures made from a variety of materials— wood, fibre, bamboo, or steel.

The Last Stand

Installation in Leopold Hoesch Museum,
Düren, Germany
15ft x 28ft x 36ft (4.6m x 8.5m x 11m)

Karen Stahlecker 1992

WITH MY INSTALLATIONS I HOPE TO EXPLORE FOR MYSELF AND INSPIRE IN THE VIEWER A SENSE OF THE SPIRITUAL ASPECTS OF THE NATURAL WORLD.

ELIZABETH STUART SMITH

Elizabeth Stuart Smith gained her BA in fine art at Liverpool University, England, where she discovered the art of papermaking, and, since 1977, has been exploring this most versatile medium. Her particular interest is to use the creation of paper and its subsequent degeneration to explore the constant change in our landscape—both geological and social. Sometimes this change is inevitable and beyond our control—volcanoes, landslides, floods; sometimes it is the direct result of human activity, or the destruction caused by the careless use of limited resources, leading to unnecessary pollution and the extinction of numerous plant and animal species.

Outside In

Granite setts covered with straw paper
25in long x 21in wide x 7in high
(64cm x 54cm x 18cm)

Elizabeth Stuart Smith 1995

I HAVE USED MATERIALS FROM OUTSIDE TO MAKE WORK TO GO INSIDE. THE GRANITE SETTS, WHICH WERE ONCE LAID IN A ROAD, NOW SIT ON A WOODEN FLOOR. STRAW, WHICH ONCE GREW IN A FIELD, HAS BEEN MADE INTO PAPER, WHICH COVERS THE SETTS.

ANNE VILSBOLL

Anne Vilsboll was a founder member of IAPMA (International Association of Papermakers and Paper Artists) and became president of the association in 1996. After studying art history and French in Denmark and France, she taught for a short time but soon became involved in the art of making paper. Between 1980 and 1989 she studied in many countries, including Italy, Japan, the United States, and France. As a painter, Vilsboll is totally aware of the importance of the raw material of a work, and this has led to a lifelong passion for craftsmanship that extends to creating handmade paper. In Denmark, she is considered to be a connoisseur of the potential of paper and the techniques for working with it.

Dance of the Yellow Atoms
4¼ft x 9¾ft (1.3m x 3m)
Anne Vilsboll 1998

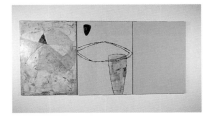

PAPER AS THE BASIS FOR A PAINTING IS IN ITSELF A METAPHOR FOR ARTISTIC CREATION. THE TOTAL DESTRUCTION AND SHREDDING OF THE MATERIAL TO CREATE ORDER FROM THE ENSUING CHAOS IS THE ULTIMATE EXPRESSION.

DAVID WATSON

Between 1979 and 1984 David
Watson studied in England, at
Liverpool Polytechnic and Kingston
Polytechnic, earning his BA in
graphic design. He followed this
with a study period with Maureen
Richardson (page 116) in
Herefordshire. He has since
studied both glass casting and
silversmithing. From this broad
base, his papermaking work
expresses his ideas in relation to
the environment and to the
practical issues of living. The artist
makes three-dimensional pieces as
well as two-dimensional collages
and huge hanging sheets, such
as the sheet shown here. This
delicate and seemingly fragile
sheet is made from grass cuttings,
supposedly of little value except
possibly as compost. As paper,
however, it has great beauty
in its color, translucency, and
tactile qualities.

lawn grass paper
17ft x 3ft (5.2m x 1m) approx
David Watson 1997

PAPER HAS BEEN A MEDIUM FOR ME FOR SOME TIME. I
LOVE ITS ACCESSIBILITY, FRAGILITY, VARIETY, BEAUTY, AND
MOST OF ALL, THOSE QUALITIES I HAVEN'T YET
DISCOVERED.

Using her skills in handmaking paper, Swiss artist Therese Weber creates works with which she tries to convey the transience of life. She qualified as a teacher in Switzerland, then study and work took her to the United States, Japan, Australia, Argentina, and China, countries in which she has also exhibited. She has learned both Eastern and Western methods of papermaking and, as a past president of IAPMA (International Association of Papermakers and Paper Artists), she has had frequent contact with other paper artists. Her work is to be found in the offices of many prestigious corporations, including Union Bank of Switzerland in Tokyo and Credit Suisse in Melbourne, Australia, as well as in her home country.

Die Form der Zeit (The Shape of Time)
39½ft x 7ft (12m x 2.1m)
Therese Weber 1992

THE SHAPE OF TIME, A STONE THROWN INTO THE WATER. CIRCLES ISSUING FROM THE CENTER AND GROWING INTO ETERNITY, FROM WHENCE THEY RECEDE AND MERGE IN THE GUISE OF A NEW VITALITY.

LOIS WILLIAMS

Newsprint is the preferred source material of Lois Williams—it is a neutral material, with which she can create a variety of shapes and structures, ideas and images. She has woven paper, shredded it, made mattresses from it and even constructed meticulous carpets from neverending strips. She has combined it with wax and cloth, fiber and wool to produce both large- and small-scale works, which have been shown in the United Kingdom, the United States, and Spain. Her pieces are to be found in the collections of the Arts Council in the United Kingdom, the Contemporary Arts Society of Wales, and with many private benefactors. Williams was born in Wales and studied at Wrexham Technical College, followed by further academic work at Manchester Polytechnic and Goldsmiths College, University of London.

Curtain
Newspaper, cotton twine
8ft x 10ft x 6in (2.44m x 3m x 15cm)
Lois Williams 1986

THE PROCESSES I HAVE CHOSEN TO WORK WITH CAN BE DIFFICULT AND EVEN PAINFUL, BUT A POINT IS REACHED WHEN THE WORKS BECOME THEMSELVES AND EVERYTHING THAT HAS GONE INTO THEIR MAKING BECOMES WORTHWHILE.

ANNA WOLF

Living as she does on the West Coast of the United States, Anna Wolf is very aware of the mingling of diverse cultural influences. She studied fine art and sculpture in Munich, and then moved to the United States, where she became involved with textiles. This lent a solid foundation to her fascination with paper, sparked as a result of her study of bookbinding. She developed an interest in marbling and in the variety of book structures and ways in which paper can be folded. The piece shown here looks at first glance as if it is made of sheets printed with Chinese characters, but it is in fact German text on Japanese and American papers, yet the overall impression is of an Oriental image.

Hong Kong Tales

45 folded units 14in x 15in
(35.5cm x 38cm)

Anna Wolf 1995

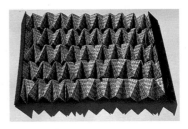

AS A BOOK ARTIST LIVING ON THE PACIFIC RIM I AM GREATLY INFLUENCED BY MANY ASPECTS OF ASIAN CULTURE, ESPECIALLY AS REGARDS PAPER AND ITS TRADITION IN FOLDING. I AM INTRIGUED BY THE POSSIBILITY OF MAKING BOOK STRUCTURES FROM MANY IDENTICALLY FOLDED UNITS.

BAST In Japanese papermaking, cleaned white *kozo* fiber that is ready to be made into pulp.

BLEED On unsized paper, ink or paint may be absorbed by the fibers, or bleed, giving a blurred or feathery edge to the writing.

CELLULOSE FIBERS Main constituent of plants that may be broken down by beating to make paper.

CHAIN LINES Wires placed across the breadth of the mold cover at ½–1¼in (1–3cm) intervals. They are at right angles to the thinner laid lines and hold them in place.

CHAPRI In Indian papermaking, a flexible screen woven from grass stems and laid on a simple mold on which sheets of paper are formed.

COLD PRESSING Process by which, after the initial pressing, sheets are put back in a press between felts and allowed to dry under light pressure for up to 12 hours. The sheets have a lightly textured surface.

COTTON LINTERS Short fibers from around the cotton seed, or boll, which are not suitable for spinning into thread for weaving.

COUCHING The process of turning out a wet sheet of paper from the mold onto a dampened felt.

DANDY ROLL A cylindrical top roller used to give a laid appearance to machinemade paper as it is being formed. It can also be used to apply watermarks.

DECKLE A detachable frame that fits over the mold and contains the paper pulp as the vatman lifts the mold and deckle from the vat.

DECKLE EDGE Feathered, slightly torn-looking edge on all four sides of a piece of handmade paper.

EBRU Turkish marbling technique, also known as floating clouds, used to create figurative, rather than abstract, patterns.

FELT Woven blanket onto which sheets of newly formed paper are turned out before pressing.

HOLLANDER BEATER Large oval tub with a cylindrical roller and sharp metal plates, in which raw materials, such as rags, are beaten with water to separate threads into individual fibers until a pulp is formed.

HORN A shelf next to the vat on which the mold is placed to drain after it is removed from the vat; also known as the stay.

HOT PRESSING Process by which paper, after the initial pressing, is pressed between hot sheets of zinc or heated rollers to produce a smooth surface.

LAID LINES Closely spaced thin wires that stretch the length of a mold cover. *See also* chain lines.

LAID PAPER A sheet of paper which, when held up to the light, has clearly defined laid lines and chain lines.

LYE An alkaline solution in which pieces of rag are boiled to break down the plant material into cellulose fibres.

MOLD Rectangular wooden frame with wire mesh stretched over the top to form a "cover" on which a sheet of paper is formed. Used with a deckle.

MOLD-MADE PAPER Paper made on a rotating mesh-covered cylinder onto which pulp is sprayed and then transferred to a moving felt before passing between rollers to remove excess water.

NAGINATA Japanese version of the Hollander beater, which replaces the cylindrical roller with sharp curved blades.

OLD DUTCH A type of marbled paper in which spots of floating color are combed into waves and then teased into curls.

pH A way of measuring acidity and alkalinity, on a scale of 0 (most acid) to 14 (most alkaline).

POST A pile of wet sheets interleaved with felts.

SIZE A water-resistant material added to paper to prevent bleeding or feathering. When size is added to the pulp this is known as internal sizing; size applied to the finished sheet is known as surface sizing.

STUFF Pulp that has been beaten until it is ready to be formed into sheets of paper; it has a slimy, slippery texture.

SU Mold cover used in Japanese papermaking.

SUMINAGASHI Japanese marbling technique meaning "the art of floating color."

TREAD In Japanese papermaking, trampling on *kozo* bark under running water to help separate the inner white layers from the outer black ones.

VATMAN Craftworker who forms each individual sheet of paper from pulp in the vat.

WATERLEAF Dried sheets of unsized paper.

WEB A continuous strip of paper as formed on a paper machine.

WOVE PAPER Paper that does not have any lines appearing in the sheet because of the way in which the mold cover has been woven.

ARTISTS' ADDRESSES

Jane Bulsgaard DANISH
Ole Olsens Allee 14
DK-2900 Hellerup
Denmark

Lucia Barata ITALIAN
Via del Lavatore 88
00187 Roma
Italy

Helmut Becker GERMAN
FlaxHemp PaperWorks Press Inc.
10835 Gold Creek Drive
R.R.4., Komoka
Ontario N0L 1R0
Canada

Neal Bonham AMERICAN
2228 N.E. 46th St.
Seattle, WA 98105
United States

Inger-Johanna Brautaset NORWEGIAN
Haugeveien 13
N-5005 Bergen
Norway

Kathryn Clark AMERICAN
Twinrocker Handmade Paper
P.O. Box 413
100 East Third St.
Brookston, IN 47923
United States

Kate Coolahan NEW ZEALANDER
57 Sefton St.
Wadestown
Wellington
New Zealand

Kathy Crump AMERICAN
1851 W. Lincoln Road
Stockton, CA 95207
United States

Jean Davey-Winter BRITISH
5 Hamilton Road
London NW10 1NV
United Kingdom

Amanda Degener AMERICAN
1334 6th St. NE
Minneapolis, MN 55413
United States

Inge Evers DUTCH
Pijlslaan 75
2014 TL Haarlem
The Netherlands

Carol Farrow BRITISH
The Coach House
5 Ringstead Buildings
Ringstead Road
Catford
London SE6 2BN
United Kingdom

Betty Friedman AMERICAN
2650 Nicol Avenue
Oakland, CA 94602
United States

Pat Gentenaar-Torley DUTCH
Churchilllaan 1009
2286 AD Rijswijk
The Netherlands

Peter Gentenaar DUTCH
Churchillaan 1009
2286 AD Rijswijk
The Netherlands

Helen Hiebert AMERICAN
1633 S.W. Skyline Blvd
Portland, OR 97221
United States

Kyoko Ibe JAPANESE
9-9 Higashinodan Terado-cho
Muko City
Kyoto 617
Japan

Eija Isojärvi FINNISH
Myllypadontie 5 A 1
00920 Helsinki
Finland

Eeva-Liisa Isomaa FINNISH
Ruoholahdenranta E 74
00180 Helsinki
Finland

Joanna Kessel BRITISH
Broadwood
Cragg Vale
Hebden Bridge
West Yorkshire HX7 5TB
United Kingdom

Naomi Kobayashi JAPANESE
Kaminaka Keihoku-cho
Kitakuwada-gun
Kyoto 601-0532
Japan

Harri Leppänen FINNISH
Piispankatu 18D
06100 Porvoo
Finland

Géza Mészáros HUNGARIAN
1118 Kelenhegyi 12–14
Budapest
Hungary

Rebecca Milner BRITISH
1E Elms Road
Clapham Common
London SW4 9FT
United Kingdom

Catherine Nash AMERICAN
1102 W. Huron Street
Tucson, AZ 85745
United States

Julie Norris BRITISH
240 Iffley Road
Oxford OX4 1SE
United Kingdom

Jacki Parry BRITISH
The Paper Workshop
Gallowgate Studios
15 East Campbell St.
Glasgow G1 5DT
United Kingdom

Jane Ponsford BRITISH
2A Arbrook Lane
Esher
Surrey KT10 9EE
United Kingdom

Prof. Dorothea Reese-Heim GERMAN
Mainzer Strasse 4
D-80803 München 40
Germany

Maureen Richardson BRITISH
Romilly
Brilley
Whitney-on-Wye
Herefordshire HR3 6HE
United Kingdom

Priscilla Robinson AMERICAN
2811 Hancock Drive
Austin, TX 78731
United States

Fred Siegenthaler SWISS
Stockertstrasse 2
CH-4132 Muttenz
Switzerland

Robbin Ami Silverberg AMERICAN
50–52 Dobbin St.
Brooklyn
New York, NY 11222
United States

Marian Smit DUTCH
Vuurtorenweg 182
1795 LN de Cocksdorp
Texel
The Netherlands

Karen Stahlecker AMERICAN
101 Hwy V-18
Vining, 1A 52348
United States

Elizabeth Stuart Smith BRITISH
Stocks Old Vicarage
Over Peover
Knutsford
Cheshire WA16 9HD
United Kingdom

Anne Vilsboll DANISH
Stryno
5900 Rudkobing
Denmark

David Watson BRITISH
Flat C
Coronation Street
Brighton
East Sussex BN2 3AQ
United Kingdom

Therese Weber SWISS
Atelierhaus
Fabrikmattenweg 1
CH-4144 Arlesheim
Switzerland

Lois Williams BRITISH
Tan y Bryn
Cefn
St. Asaph
Denbighshire LL17 0HG
United Kingdom

Anna Wolf AMERICAN
Bookworks
2214 Los Angeles Ave.
Berkeley, CA 94707
United States

INDEX

ACKNOWLEDGMENTS

The publishers would like to thank the following for the use of their photographs:

p136: Martin Barlow

p137: Noel Brown/Oriel Mostyn

p46: Britstock-IFA

pp122/123: Carlo Carnevalli

pp6/7, 59: Torben Dragsby

p11: e.t. archive

p12: Mary Evans Picture Library

p125: Richard Goet

pp126/127: Anne Gold

pp116/117: John Hatfull

pp 4, 66/67: Geir S. Johannessen, Fotograt Henriksen a/s, Bergen

p59: Joker Foto: Design

pp56/57: Shoji Kita

pp98/99: Arika Koike

pp114/115: Alma Larson

pp102/103: László Szelényi

pp94/95: Jouko Leskelä

pp90/91: Ei Oiwa

p49: Panos Pictures

pp32/33: Dieter Spinnler

pp112/113: Richard Weltman

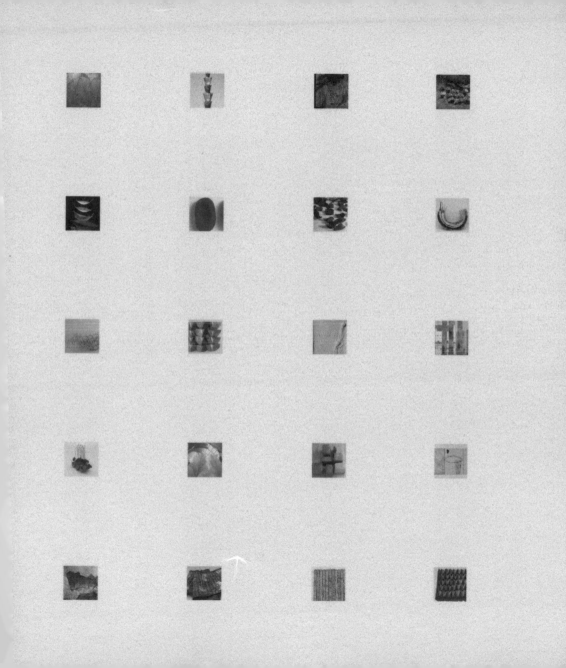